Color your life
with the color of your childhood dreams
Coloring & Poetry book

Vol.1

By Karen Pink

Color your life with the color of your childhood dreams Vol.1

Published by Kamolwan Penaram
Cover design and illustration by Karen Pink

First edition published in 2023.
Typeset and distributed by Karen Pink

ISBN: 9798391153610

Sirikamon.bkk@gmail.com

Karen Pink (Kamolwan Penaram) asserts the moral right to be identified as the auther of this work.

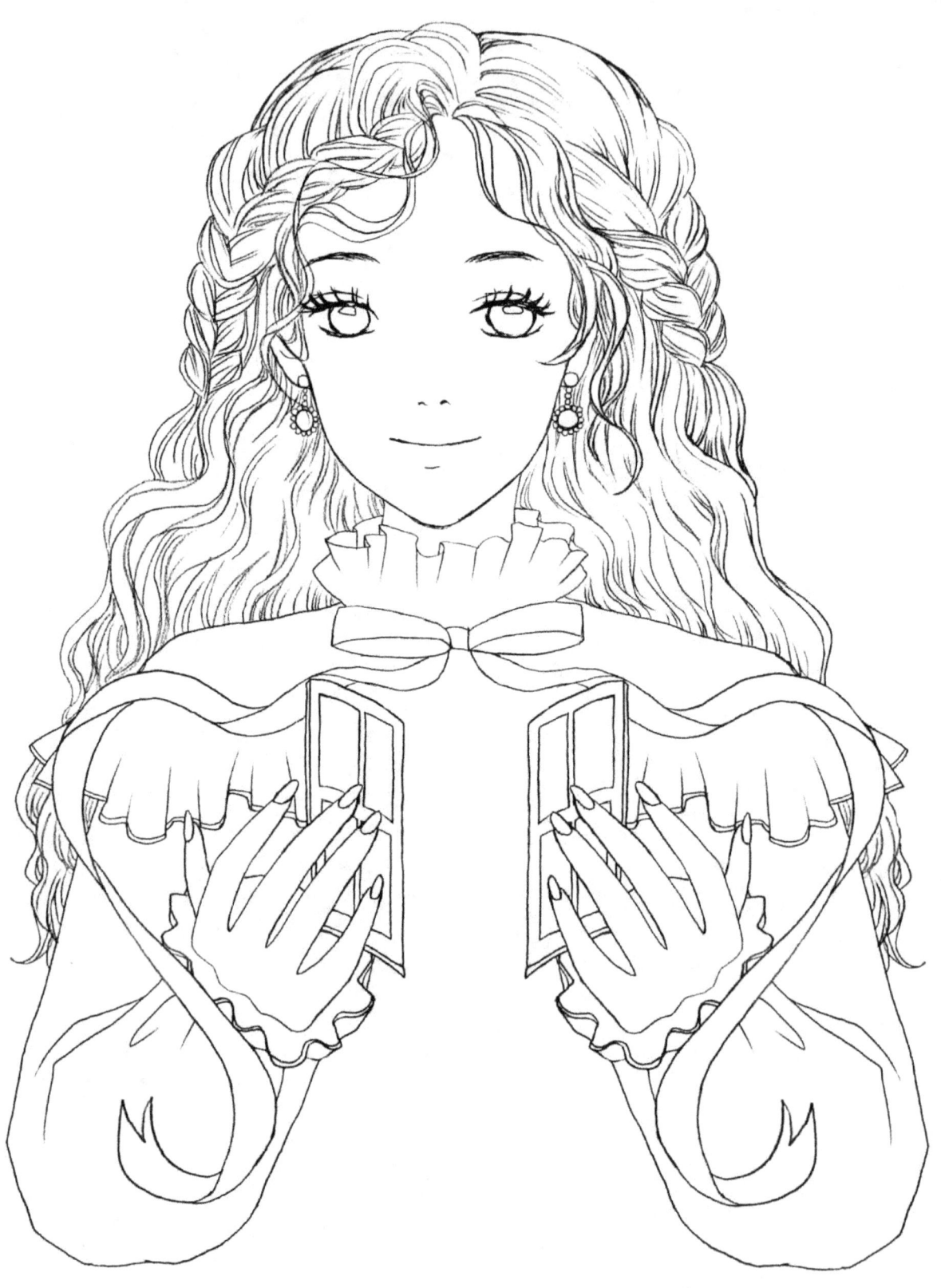

What color did you see in your dreams?
Let's grab the opportunity
to revive that faded color with this book!

Contents

Introduction

Humans are bizarre creatures.

When we were children, we used to say, "I want to become an adult as soon as possible," but when we actually grow up, we think, "I want to go back to being a child."

I think most people feel that way. There were times when I felt that way too.

But when I dug into my heart, I found my dream.

The dream is a hidden and forgotten dream, but it still sparkles even when I close my eyes.

Then I awoke from my preconceptions and found the purpose of life, both in my dreams and in the real world.

Now I don't think I want to go back to being a kid anymore because my childhood has been revived.

Even though I'm clumsy, I'm trying to make my life full of fun and happiness with my own hands, so the boring days are getting more and more colorful.

I would like to convey that feeling to everyone, so I started writing this book.

This is a book that I made entirely by myself, so I probably made some mistakes, but I tried my best to write every word and every page, and I hope that you will enjoy it even a little.

Karen Pink

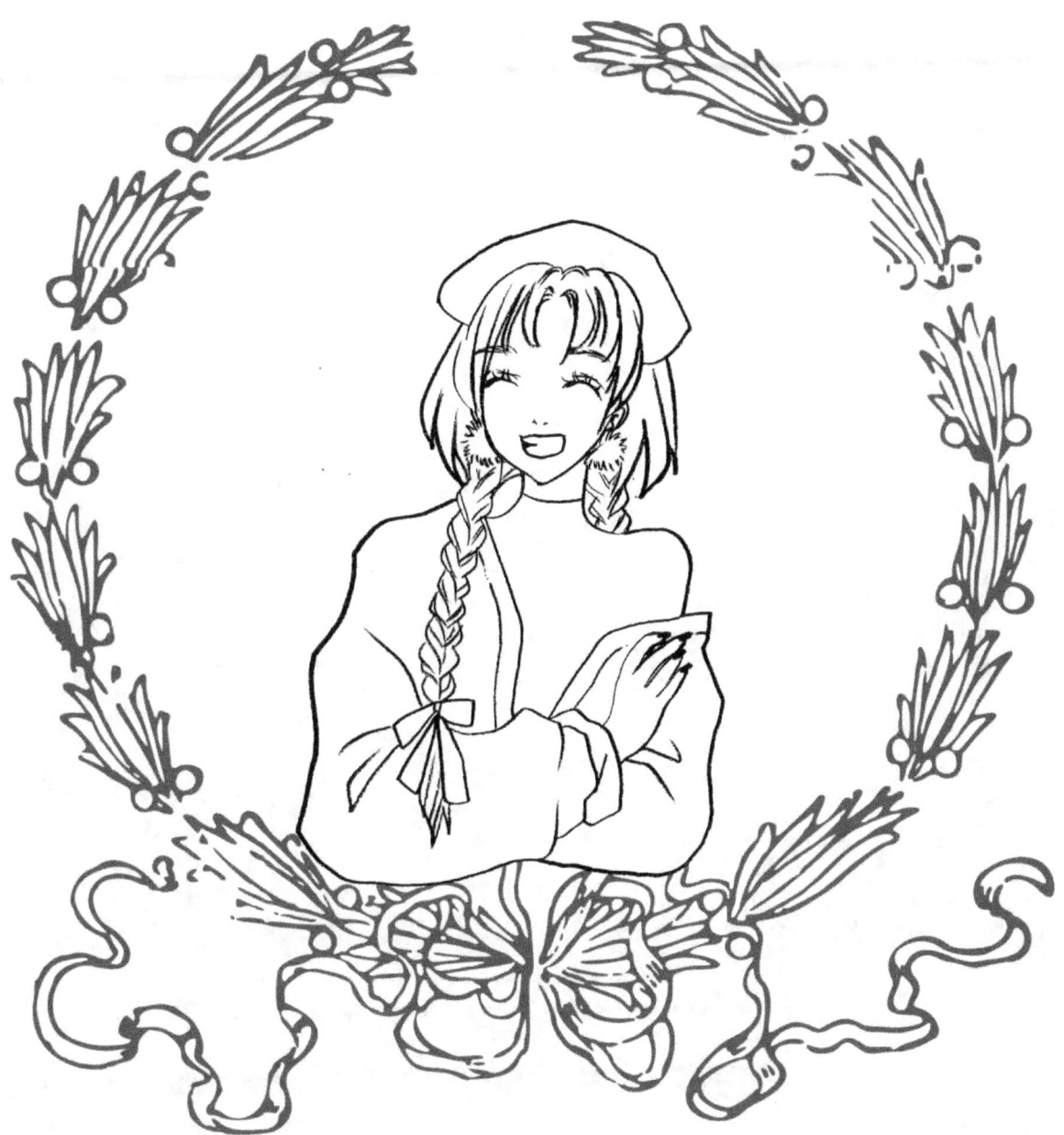

.ₒ .▪ °★▪.▪☆▪ °ₒ .

Coloring & Poetry

Let's look at the dream color and paint it
while opening our eyes to reality.

.ₒ .▪ °★▪.▪☆▪ °ₒ .

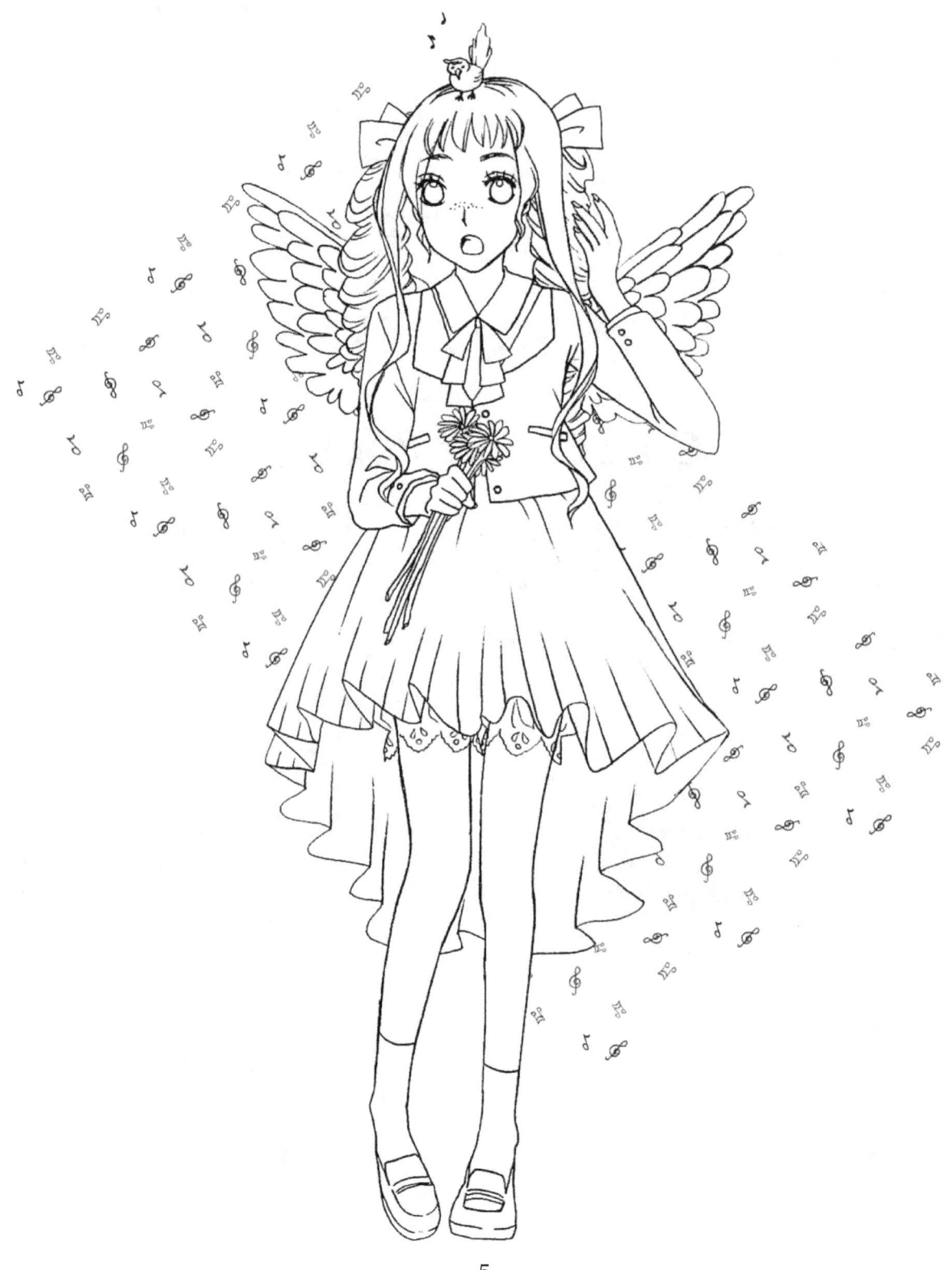

My mind is magical
It can manifest without incantation
My heart is flyable
It can soar without wings

The sun belongs to no one.
Even if someone wants to own the sun, they can't.
The sun is just there to give you warmth,
And it shines so that everyone can live.
I want to be the sun.
I'm not only pretty,
Nor can I be occupied.
I am a necessary presence in the world with a dazzling light.

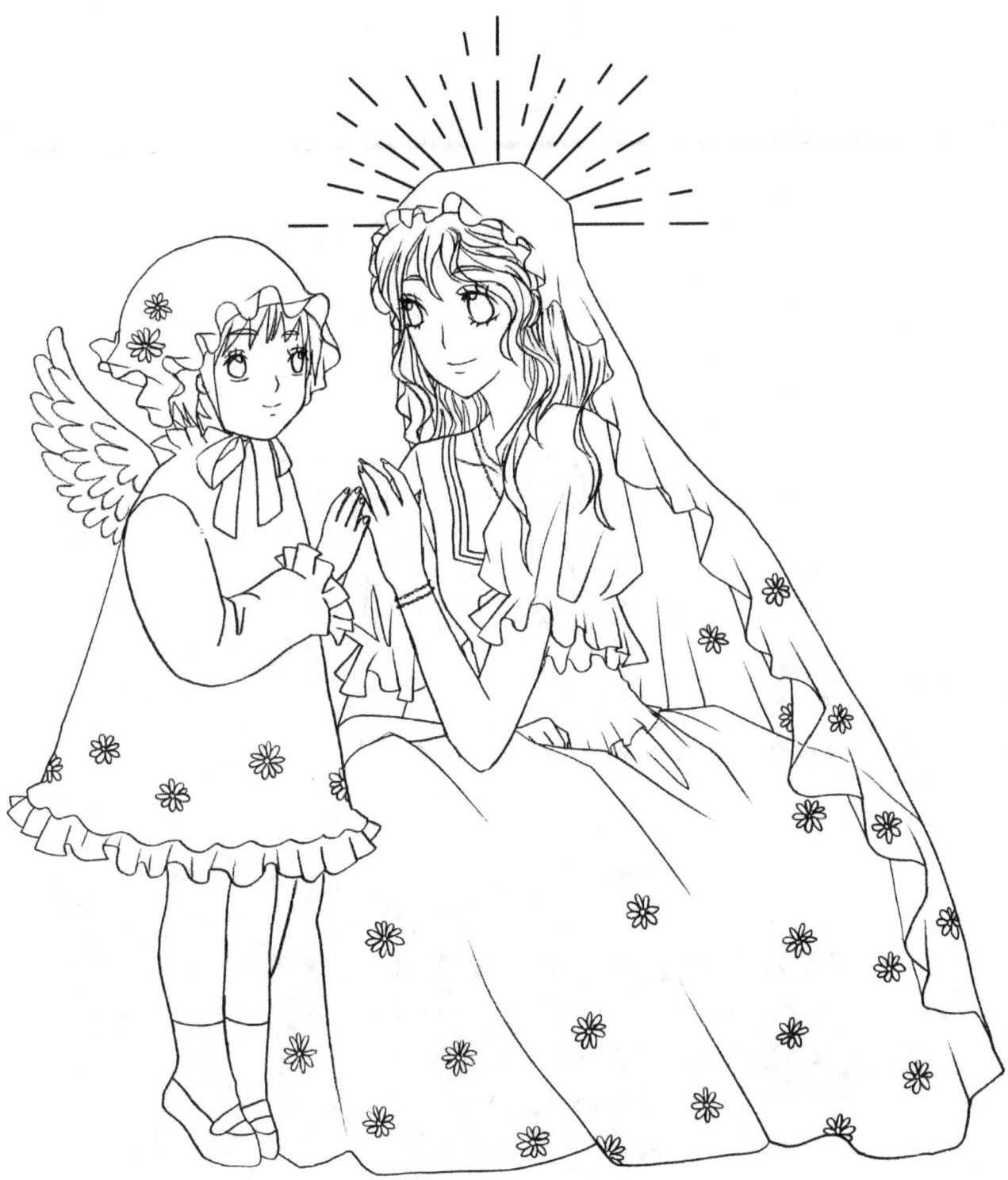

8

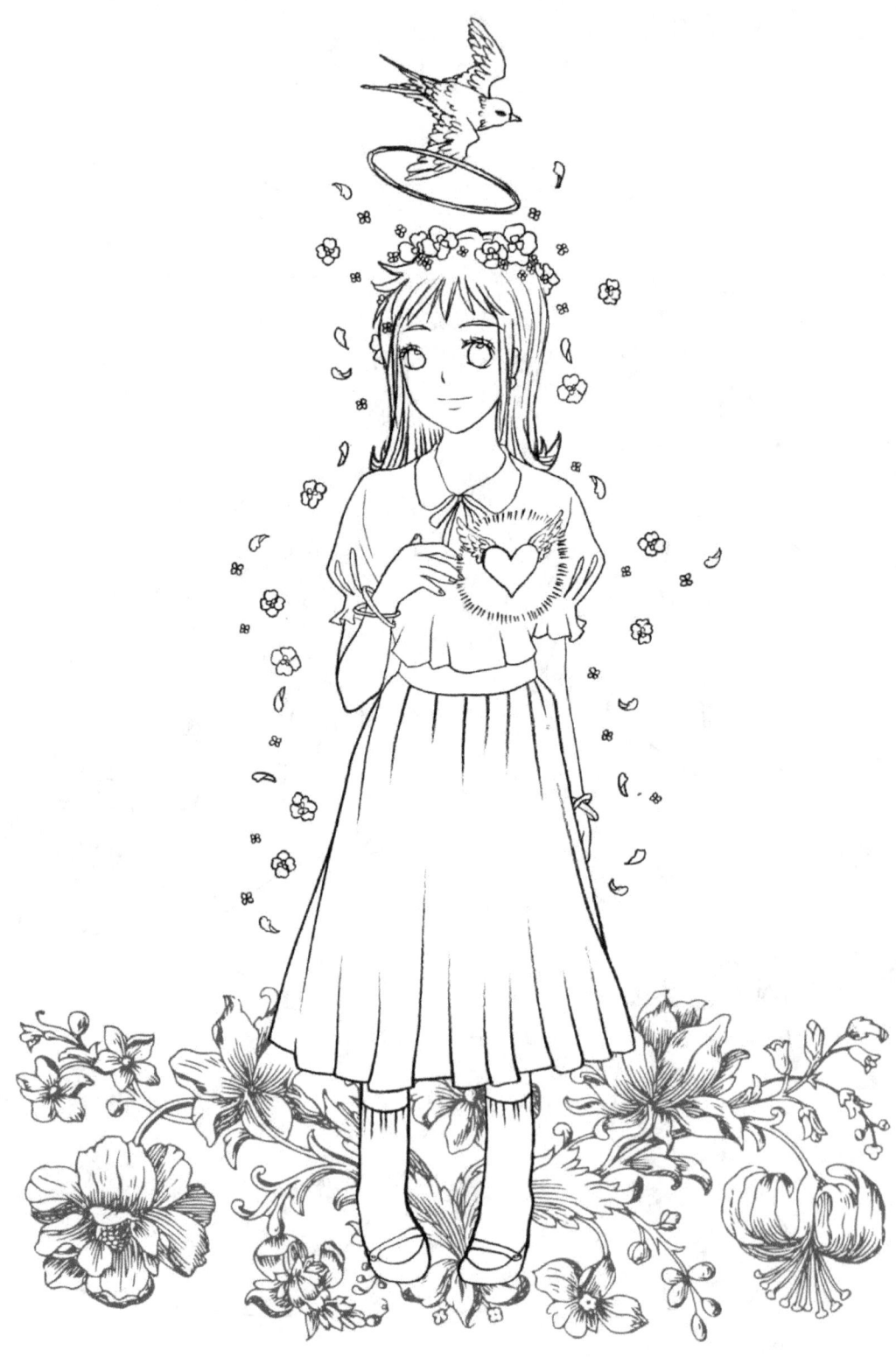

Spread your wings,
Fly to your heart.
Bring along hope and happiness,
Let's travel to today and tomorrow.

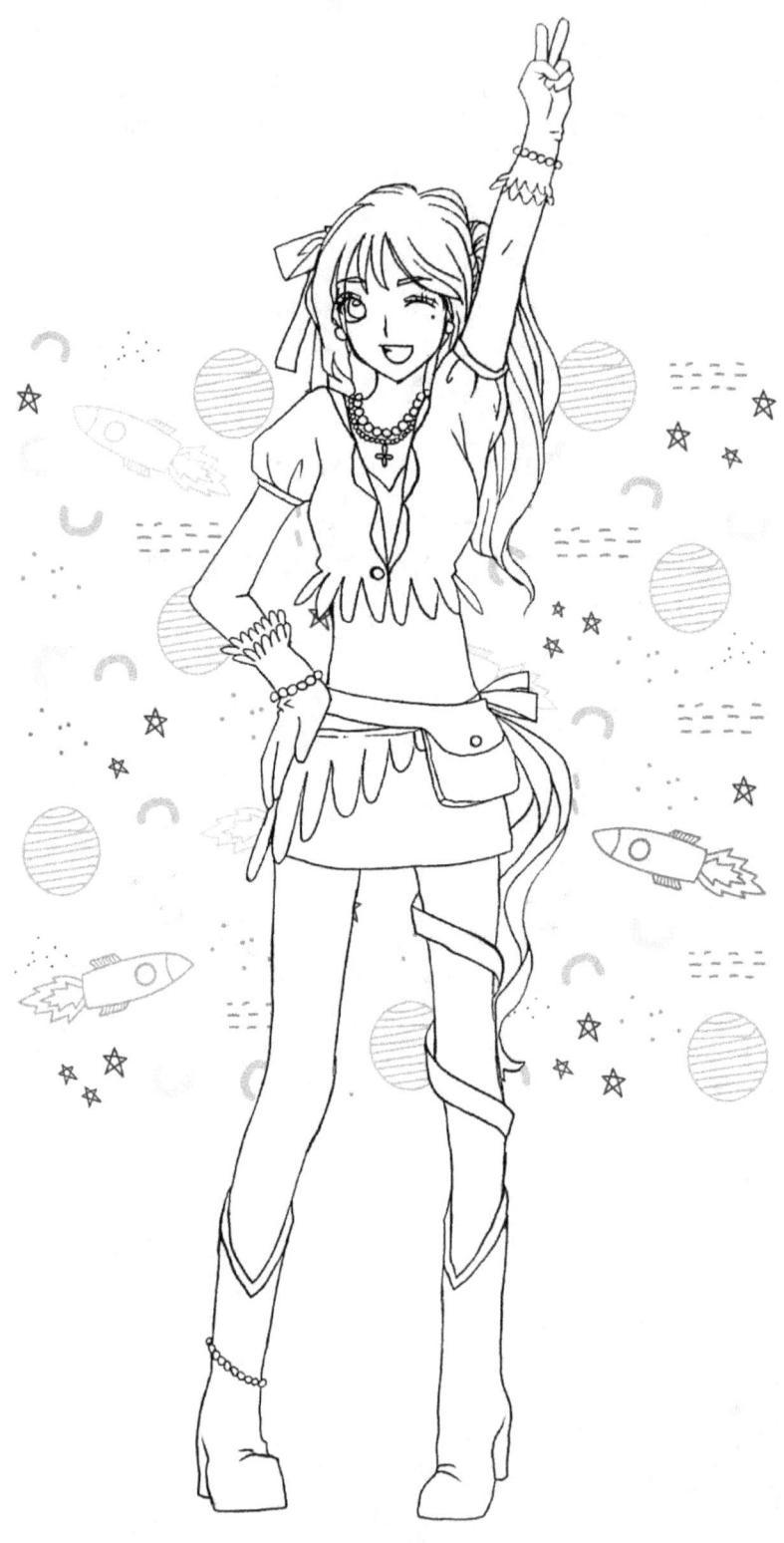

"You'll be fine"
is like a magic word with mysterious powers.
I'm an ordinary person,
But I feel strong enough to create a beautiful rainbow.

The only person who knows best
how hard you've worked so far is Yourself.
So, I want you to be kind to yourself.
Don't deny yourself.
Send love to whoever you are.

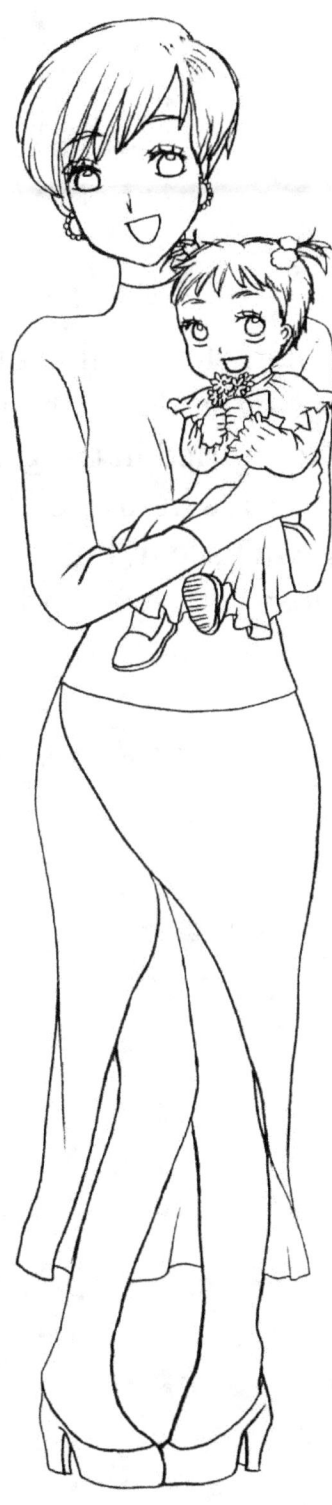

14

What I've been looking for all along hasn't sunk in the sea,
Not hidden by clouds,
Not buried in the ground.
It's in my heart.
You can't see it, but it's shining.
Now close your eyes and take a look.

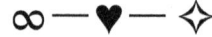

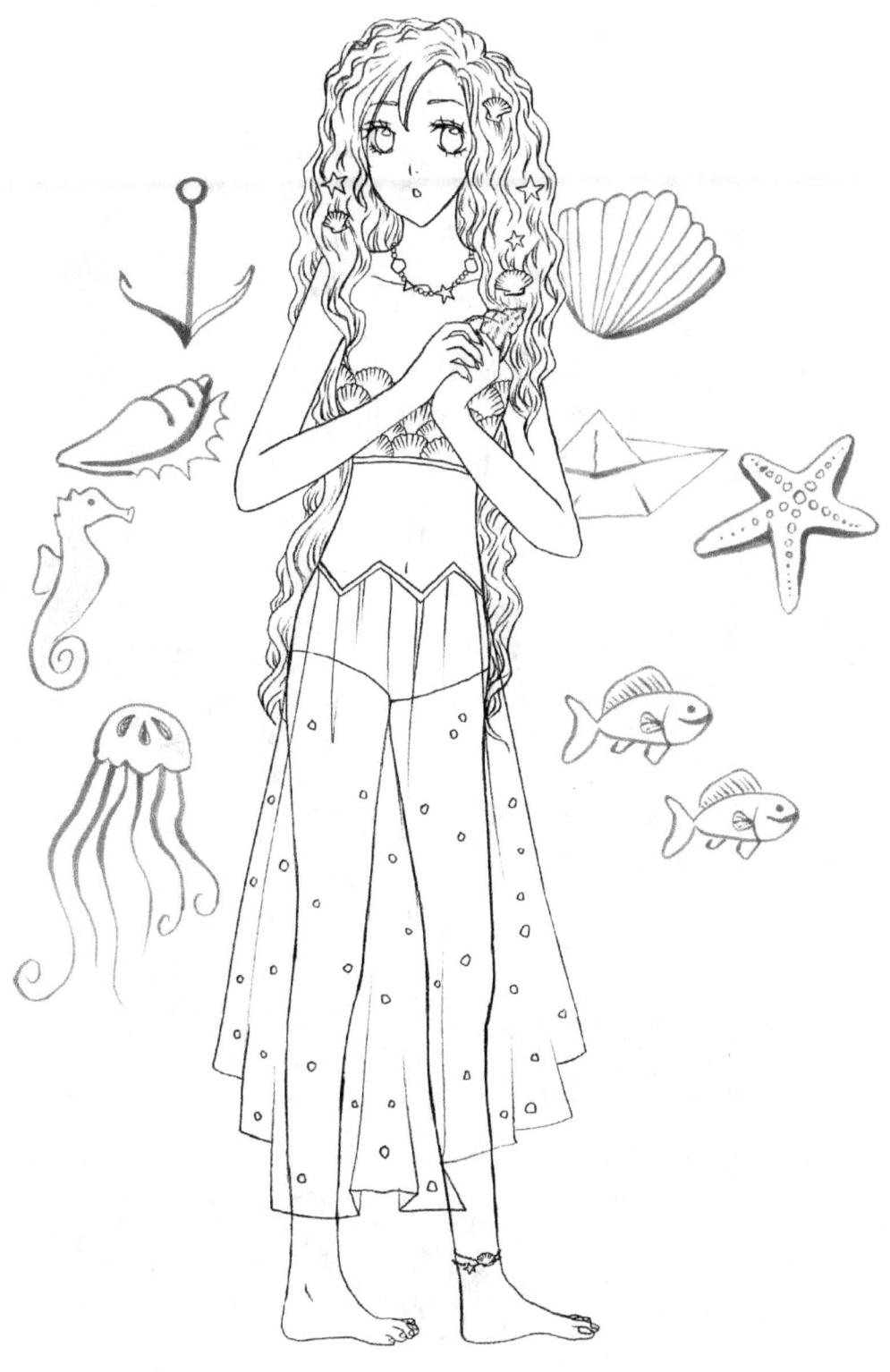

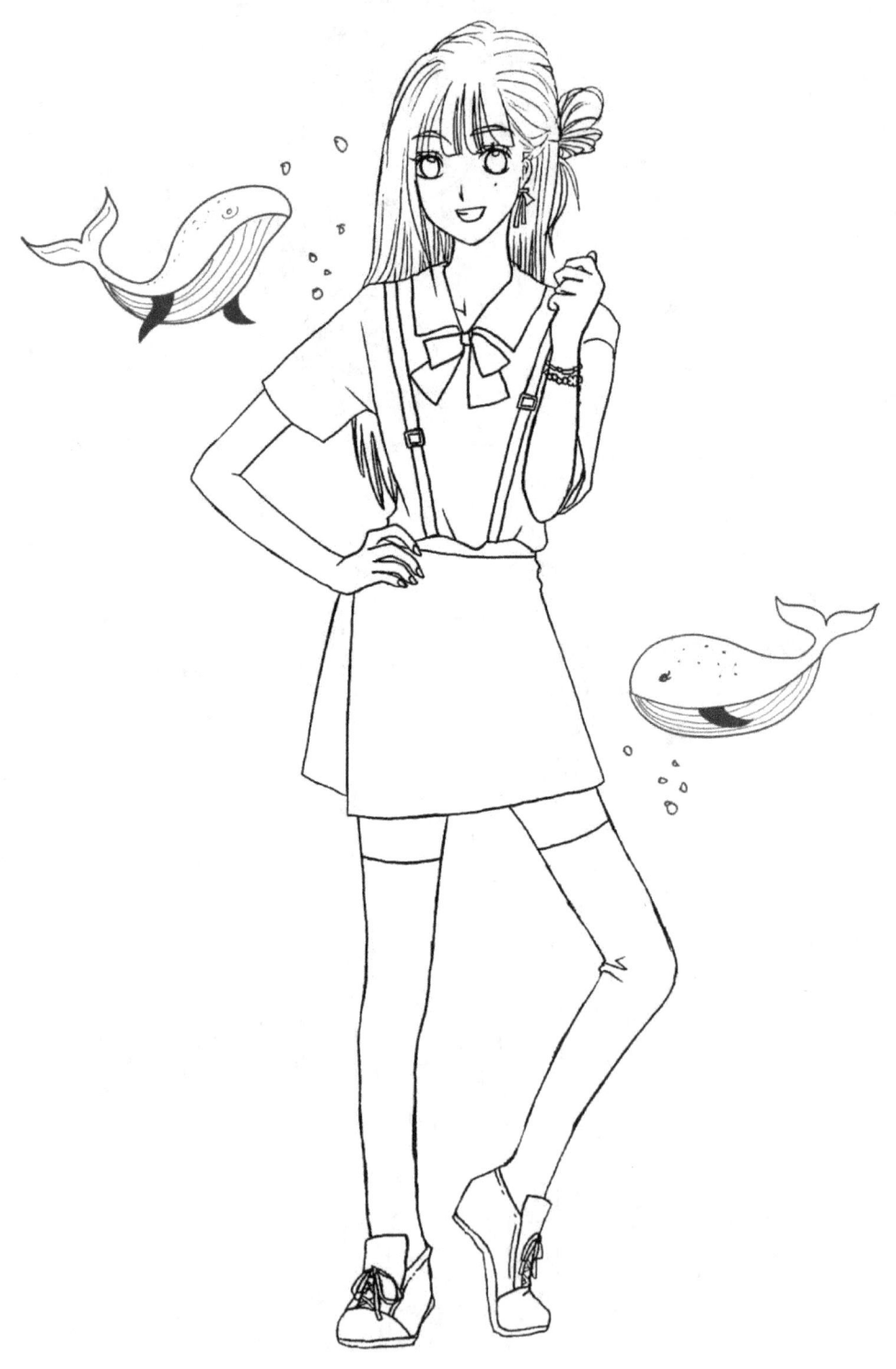

Music is played in my head.
The universe is in my heart.
Love is carried by the blood.
A miracle travels from person to person.
Everything goes around and around.

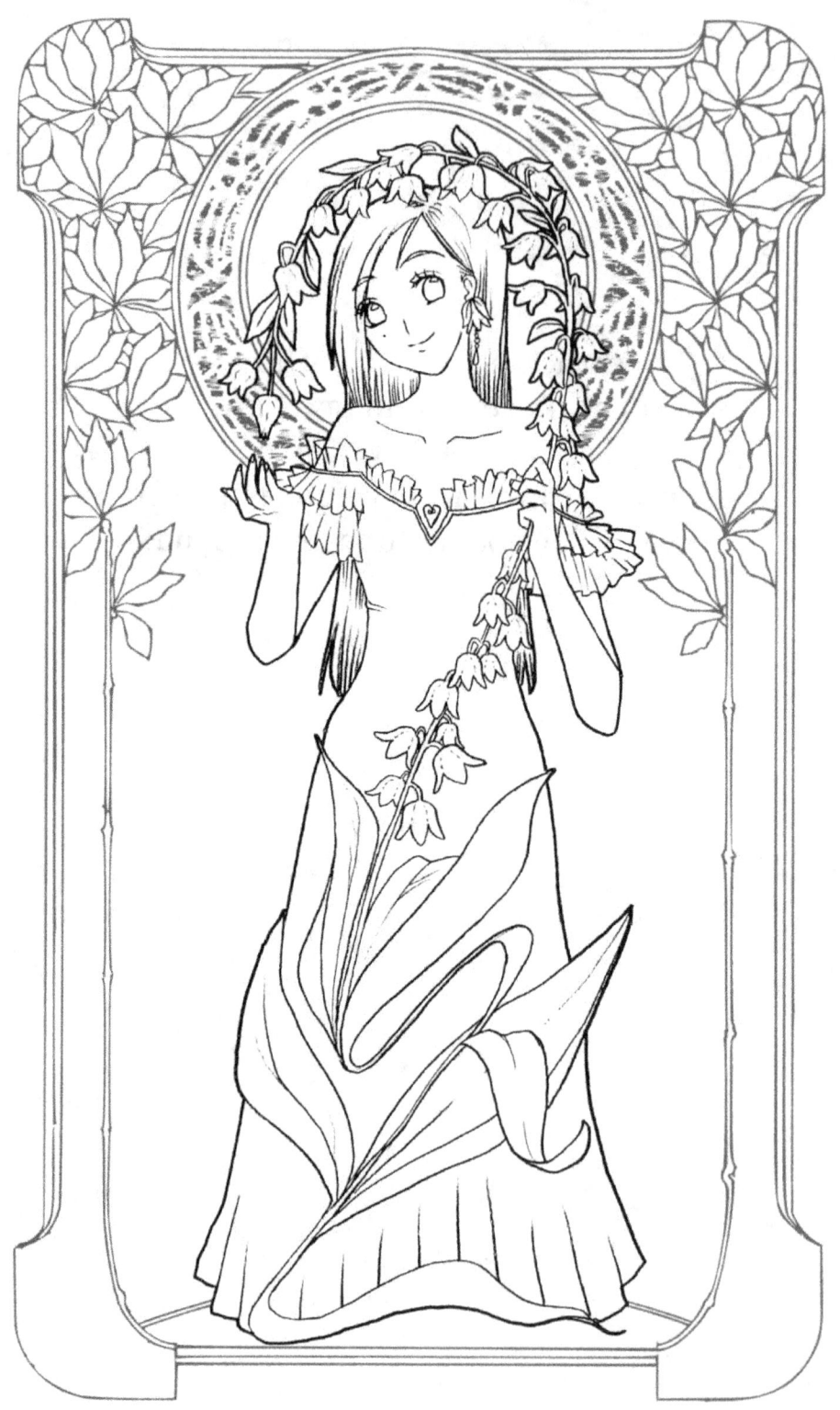

"Wild flower"
Flowers blooming in the wilderness
A small life with the colors of dreams
Freedom is in their breath
They admire the warm sunlight
And live without fear of pouring rain or snow.

"The sound of tears"

The sound of tears is silent.
Even if you listen carefully, you can't hear anything.
Actually, it's not about using your ears,
It's about using your heart.

To hear the sound of tears,
Feel them with your heart.
I think they're for understanding people
And sharing feelings.

The sound of tears is silent,
But whenever you have tears in your eyes,
Please let me hear them.

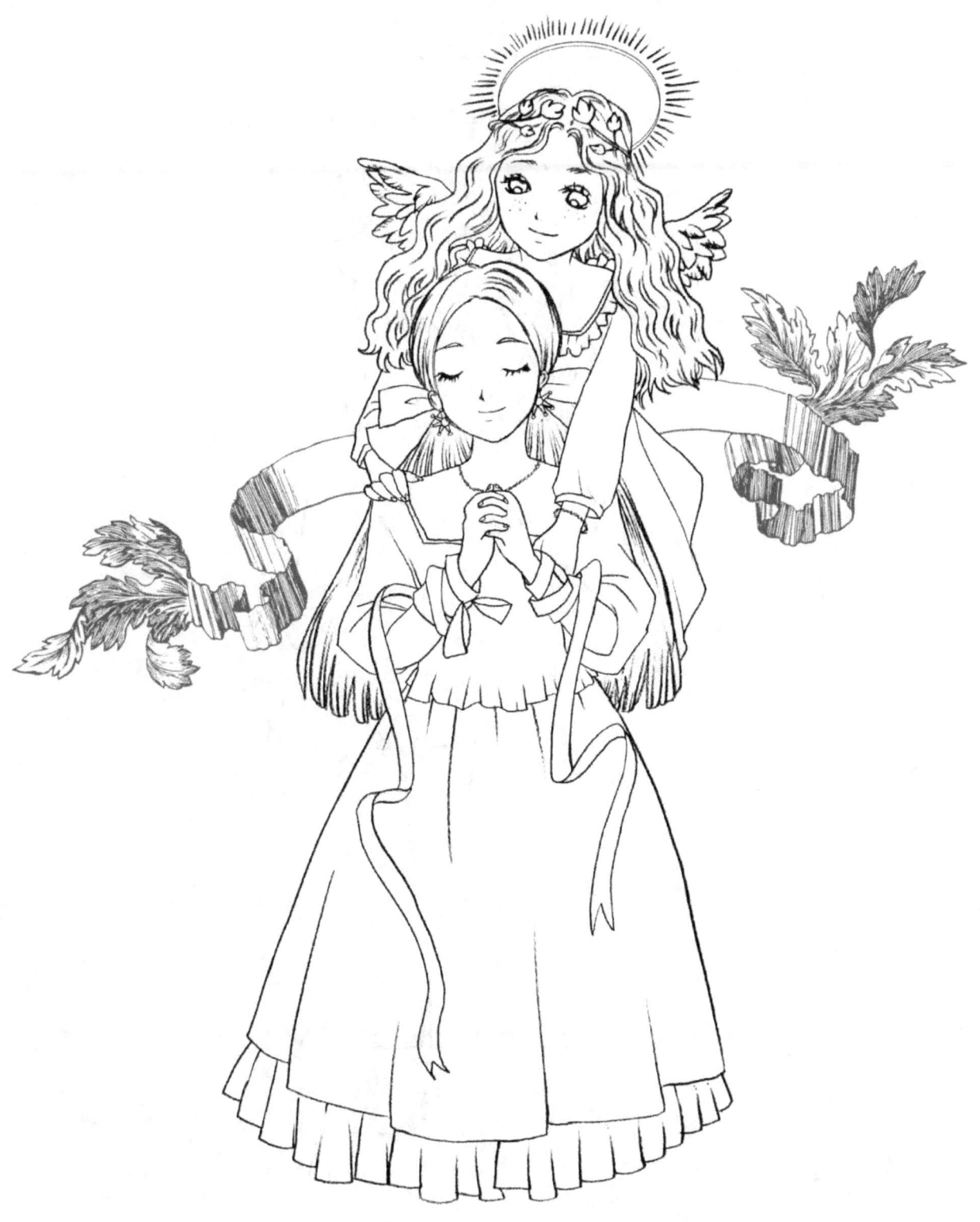

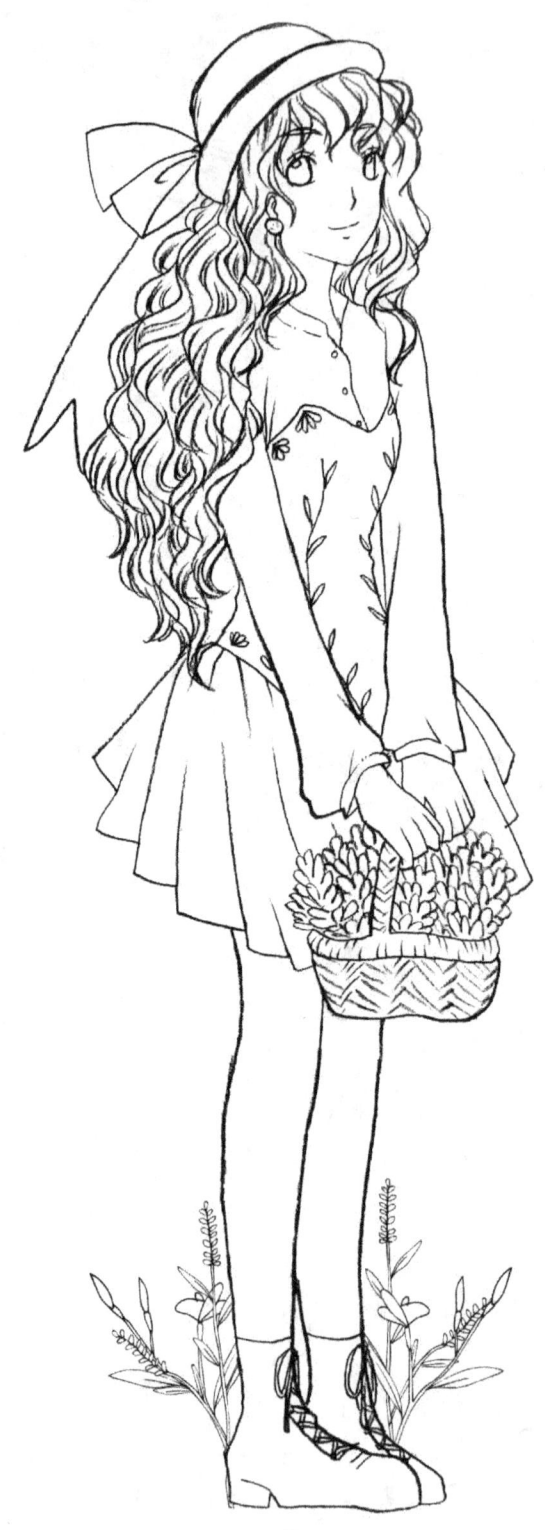

I want to meet you
In the land of dreams,
So I deliver short-lived words
Through the sea of silence.

What is reflected in your eyes?

dreams
                    light from the window

                                a phantom

a dark room
                        purple flowers

a distant rainbow
                                        blurry sunbeams
                    your beloved people

a distant illusion
            your scratches
a lonely room

        faded light
                        his or her smile
            the elementary school classroom
        your mother and father
your dreams

Are they in reality?
Anyway, my eyes are reflecting dreams.

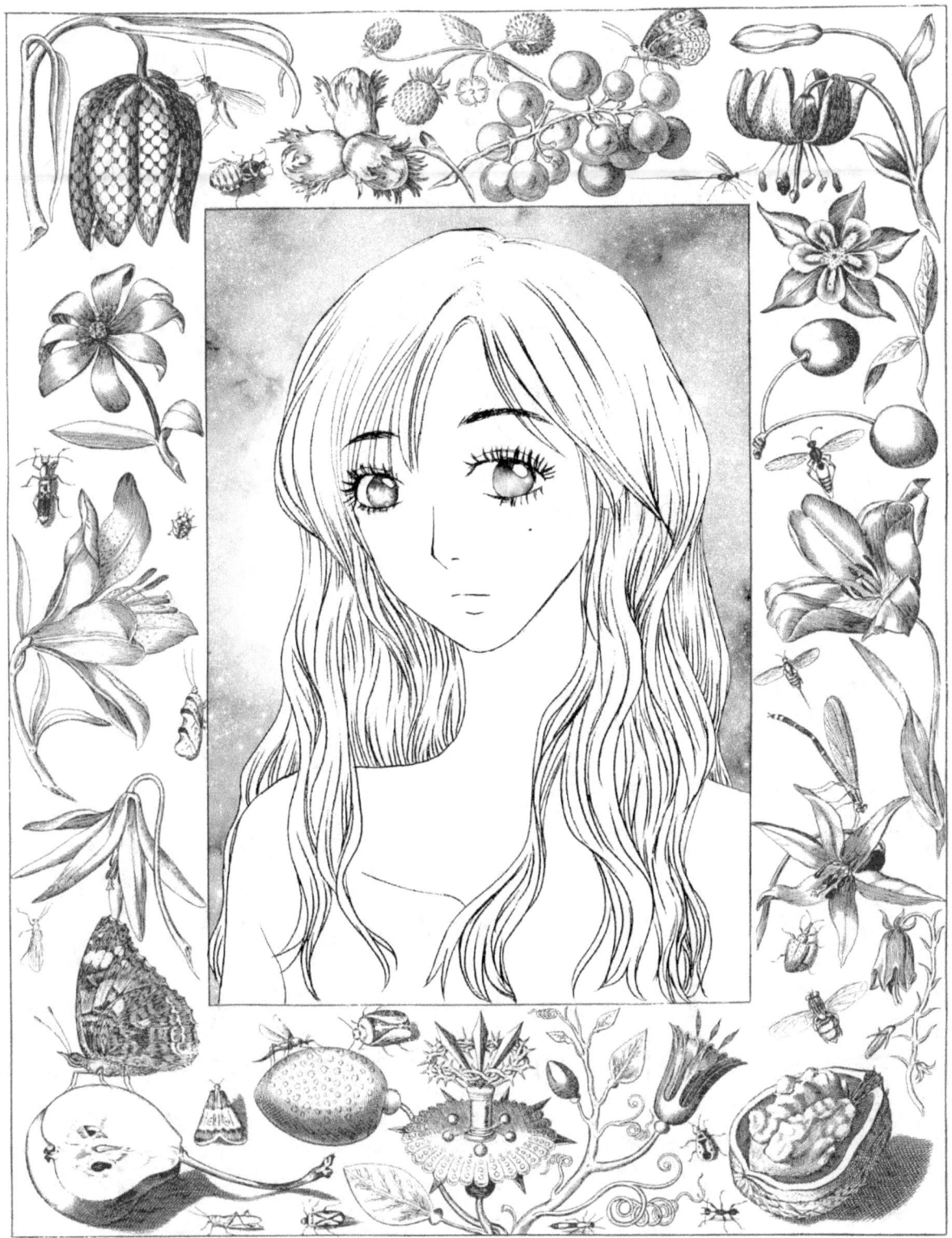

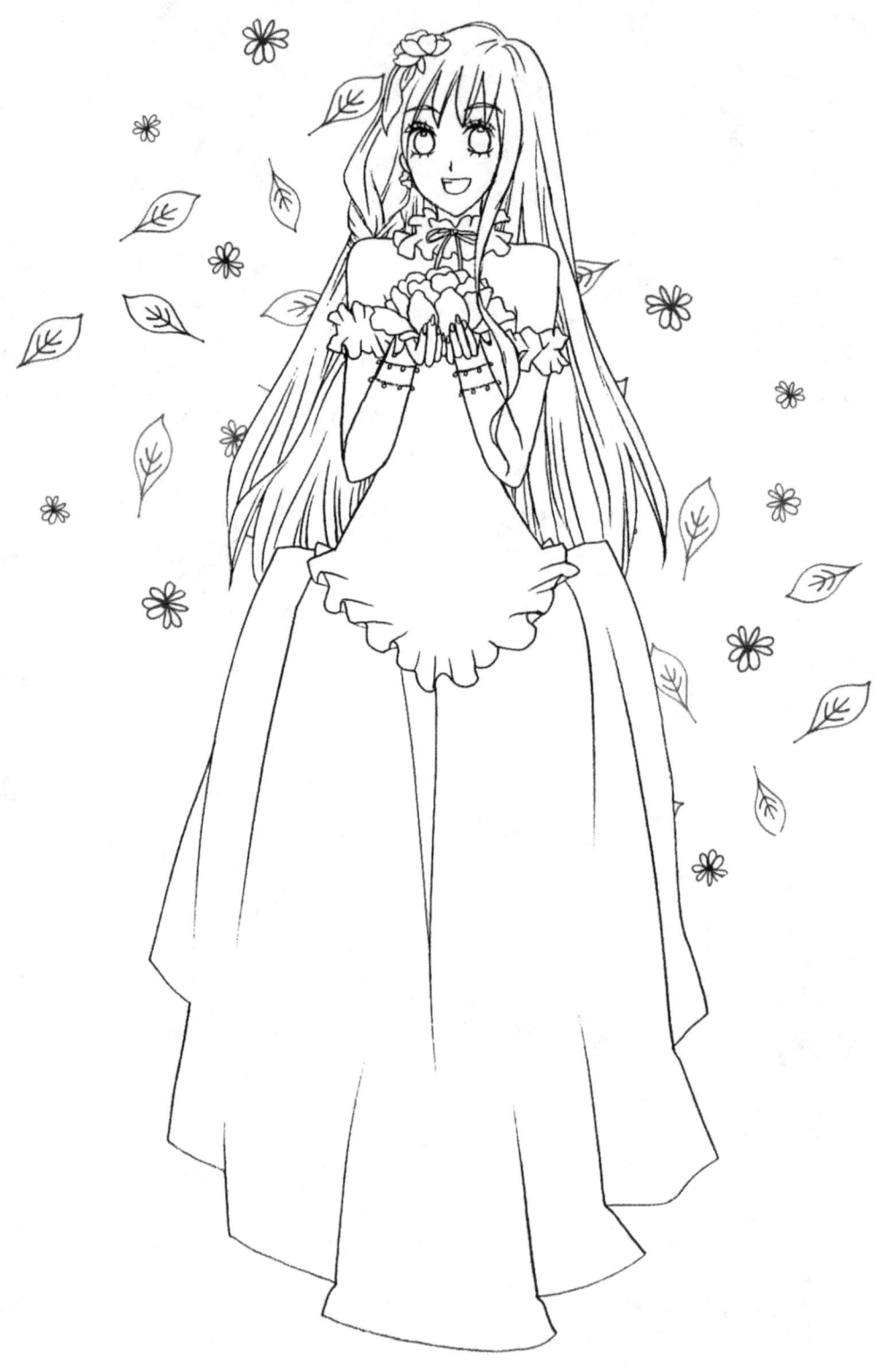

People say, "Dreams are just dreams."
I say, "Dreams are the beginning of reality."

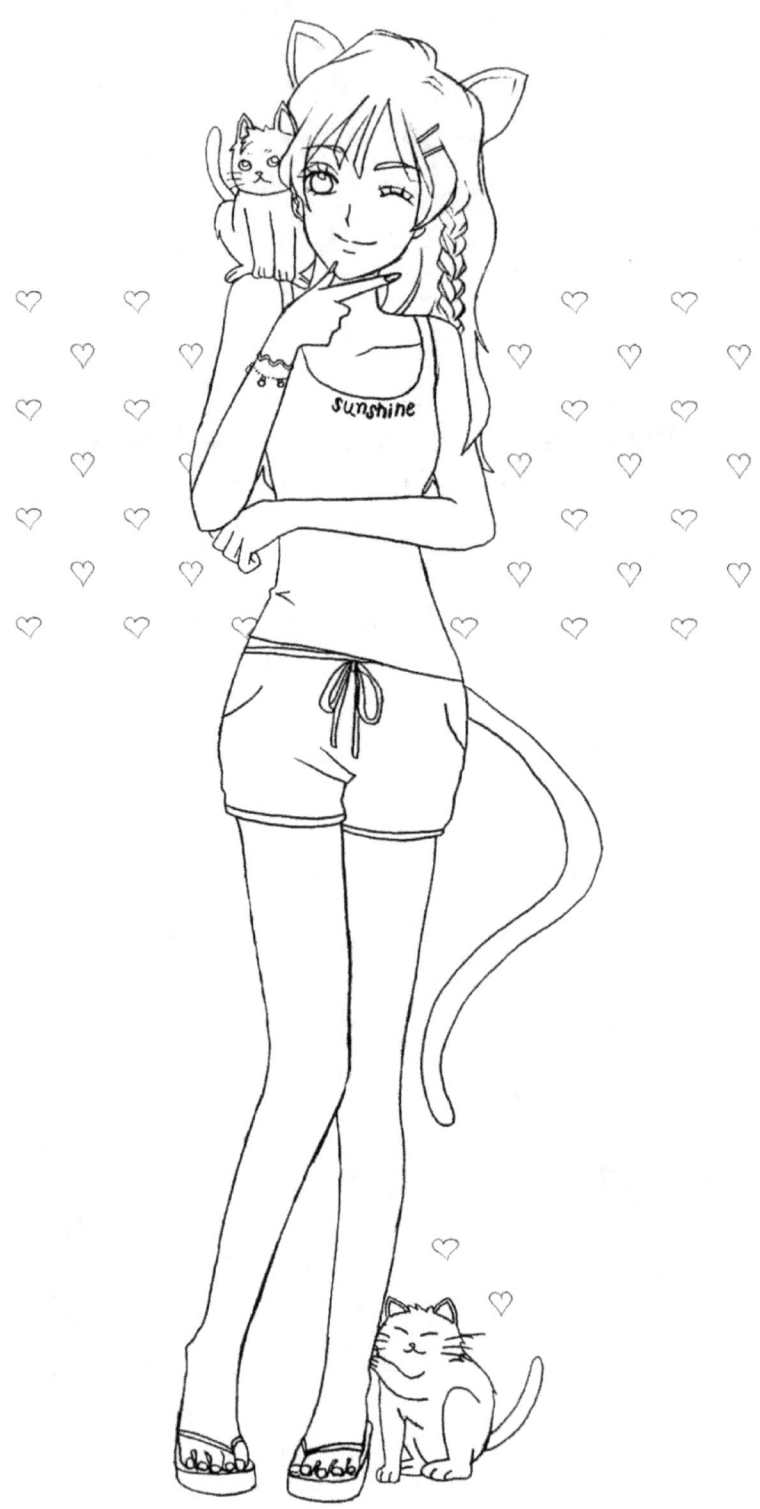

Happy moments make you want to live longer.
Sad moments make you wonder what you're living for.
Therefore, I believe that life should be lived for happiness.

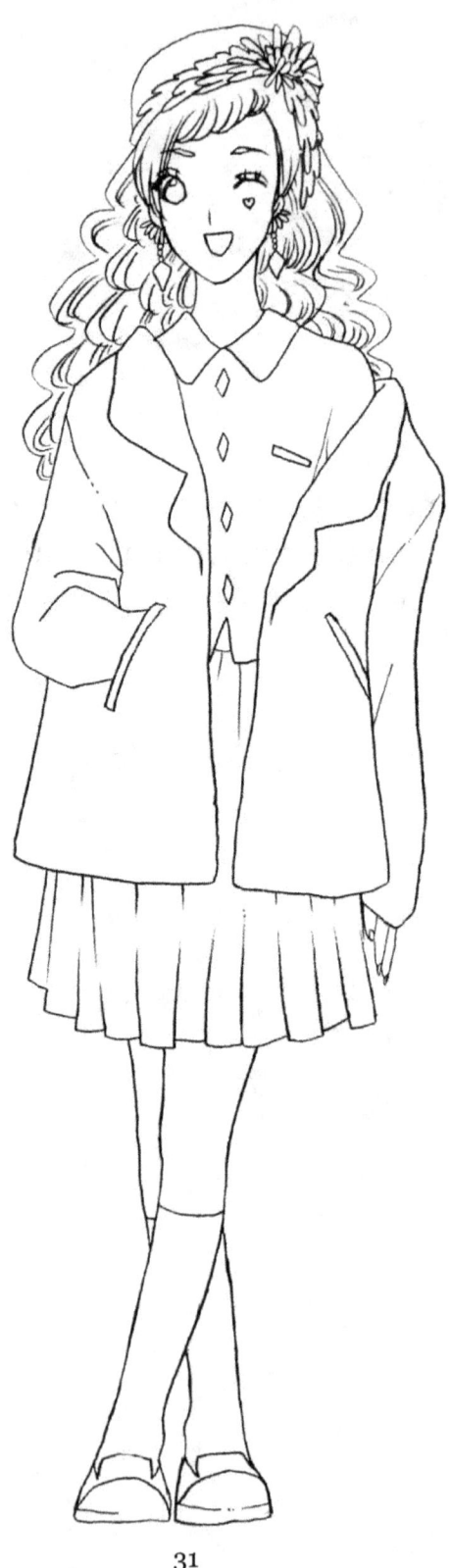

Kindness is strength.
Especially, being kind to yourself.
Not just anyone can do it.
And it doesn't get any easier as you get older.
So let's make it a priority to be kind to ourselves.

Dear the distant star,
Will you hear my wish?
I want pink, purple, and blue flowers
To beautifully decorate the world
With many flowers and various colors.
Besides, I want to gently color everyone's hearts
With silver and golden glitters.
This is my only wish.

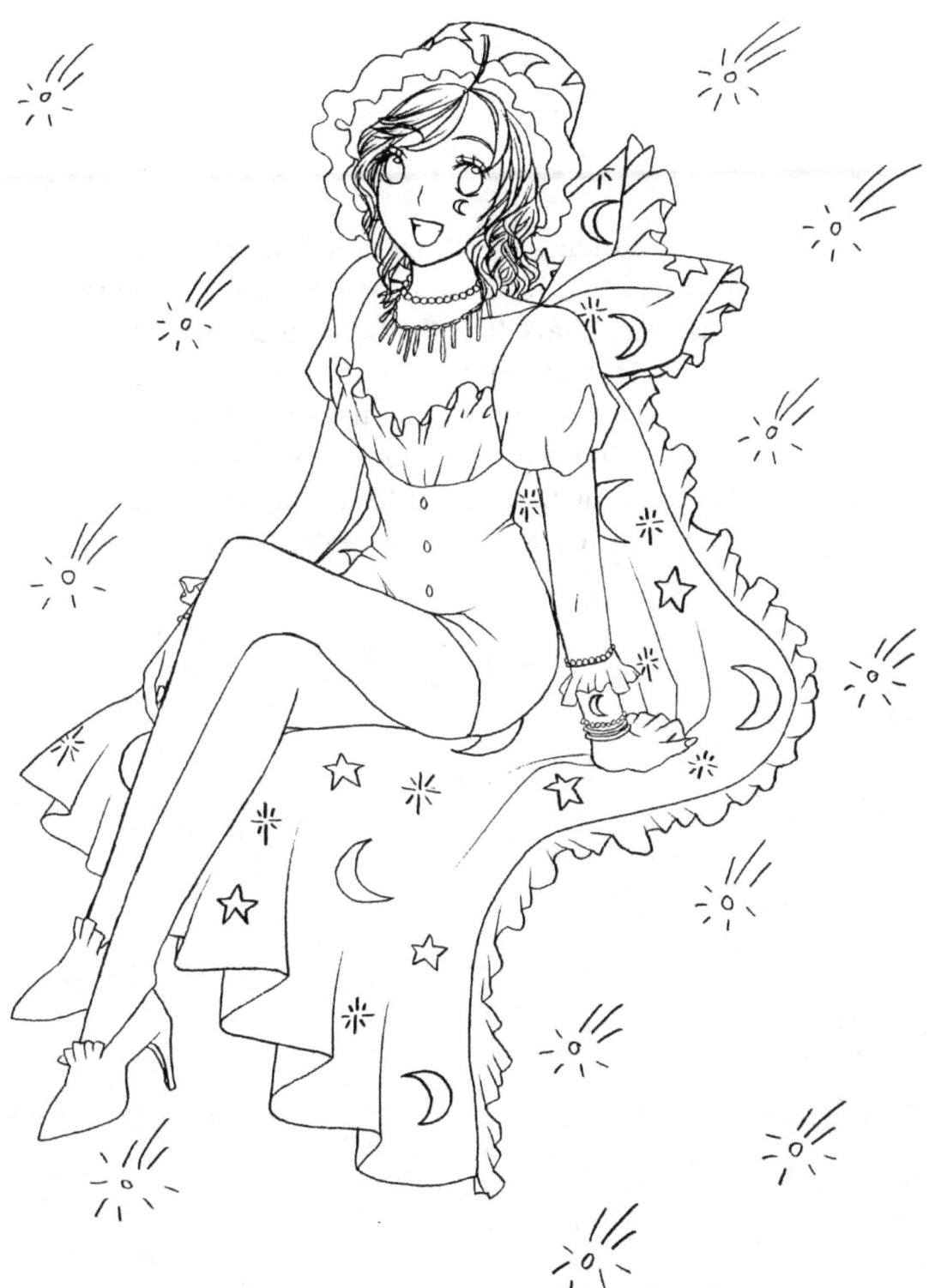

Humans aren't my only friends.
Animals, cuddly toys, and plants are also my friends.
Moreover, I have friends that adults can't see!
Like little fairies in the forest,
And scary monsters under the bed.
At dawn, the sun says "Good morning" to me.
At night, the moon says "Good night" to me.
I have a lot of friends every day!

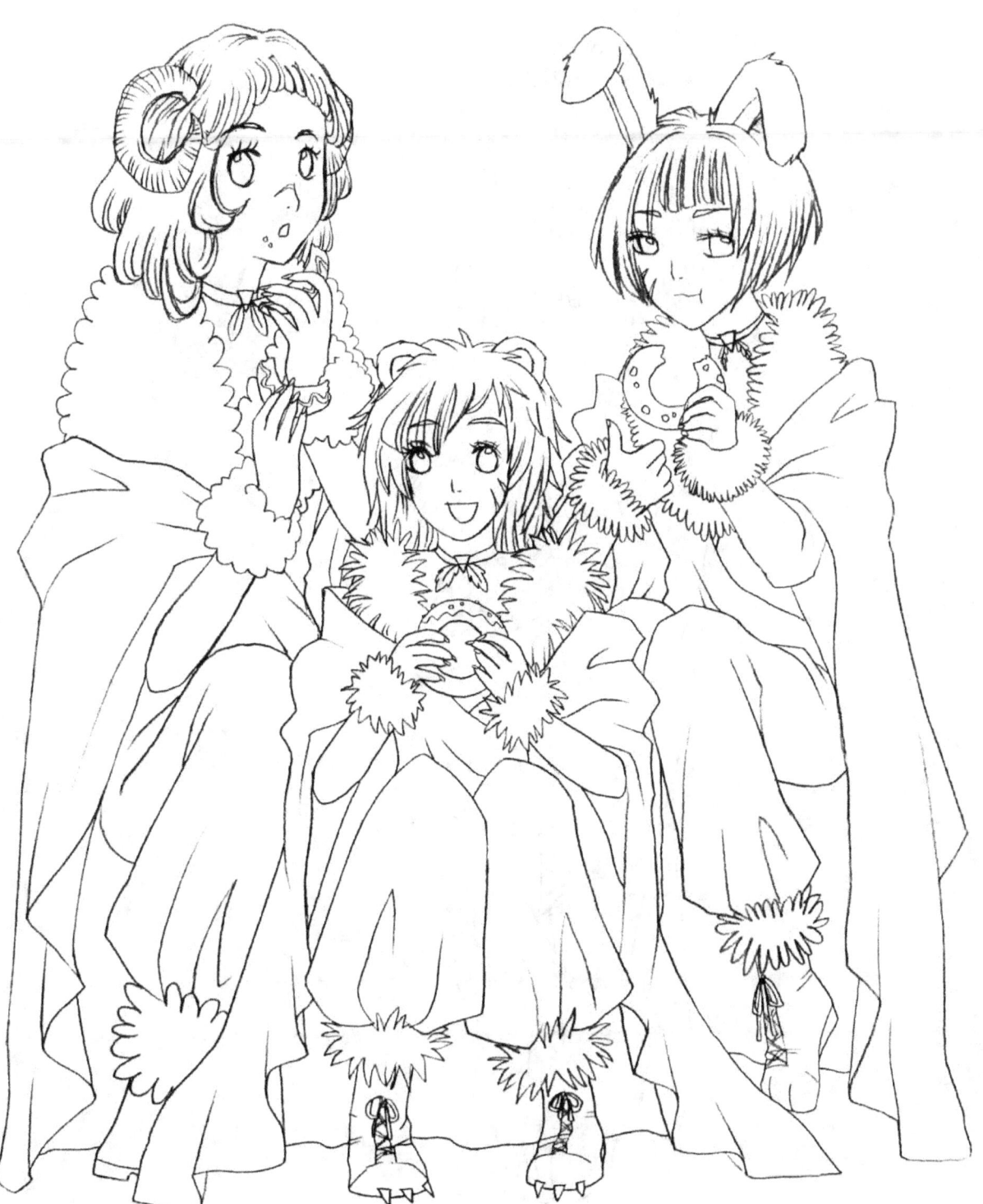

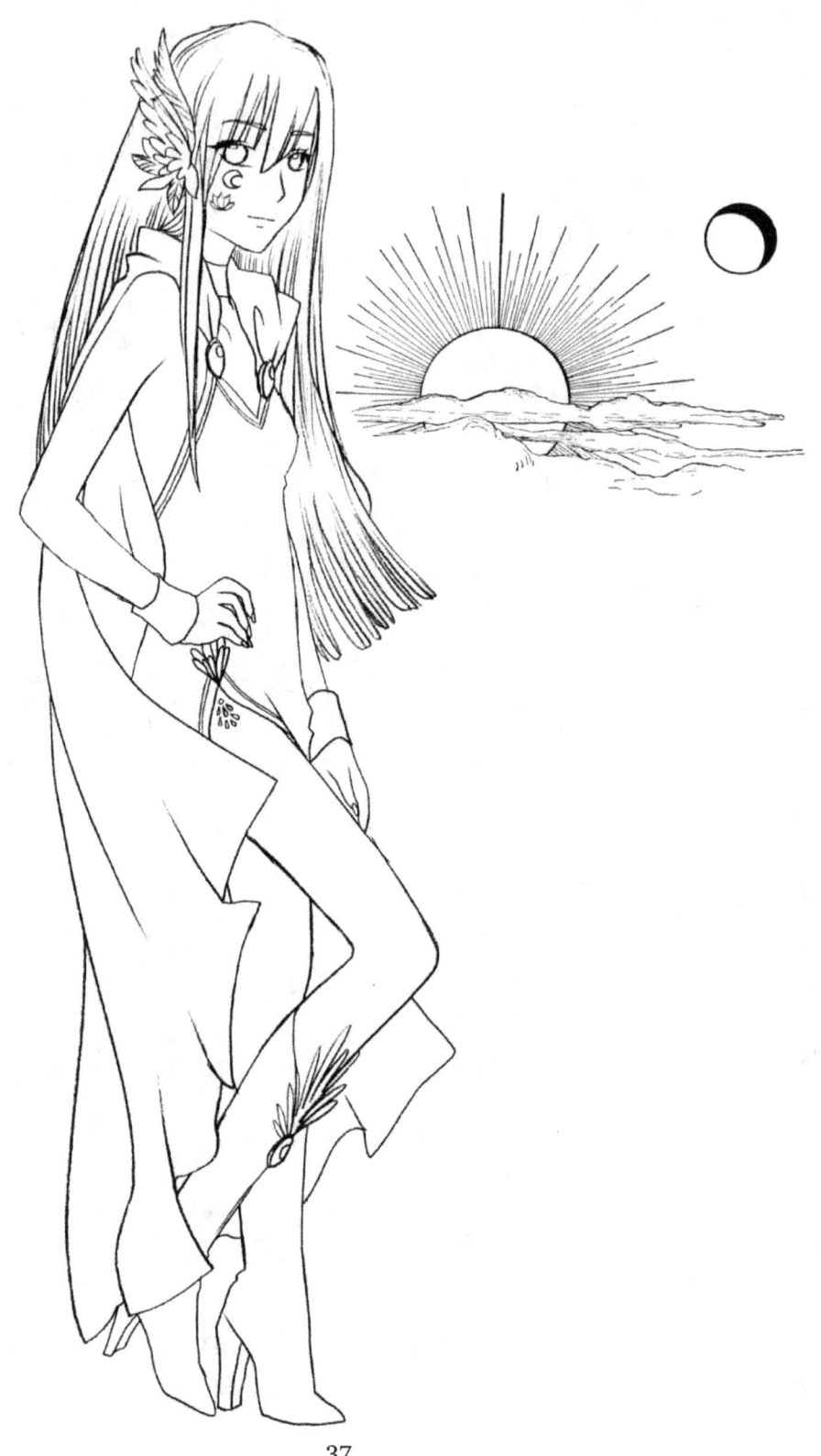

A sword isn't a tool for hurting.
A sword should be used for protection.
Using a sword, what we need isn't only strength.
Before handling any tool,
We must use our brain
And also our heart.

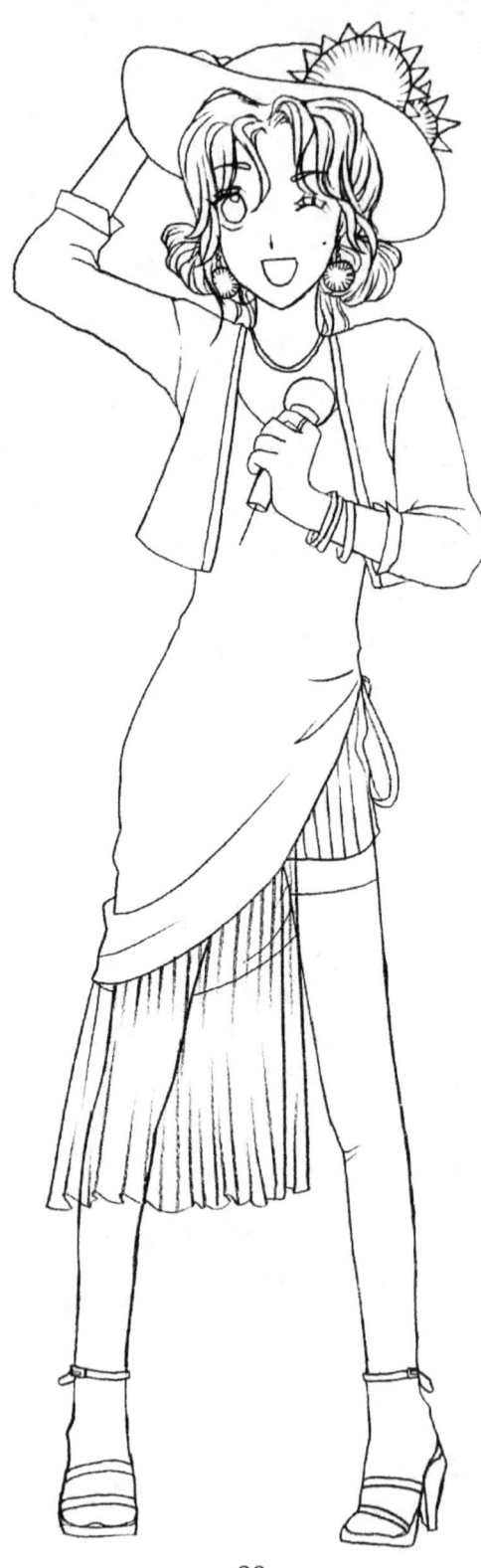

I dance alone
In the dimension no one can see
My soulful eyes spark
The sky speaks to me
With the sweetest words
They all become the sparkle in the universe

When you lose your compass,
Please don't cry
Look up at the night sky
Listen to the voice of your heart
The stars will guide you gently.
I'm sure you'll be fine.

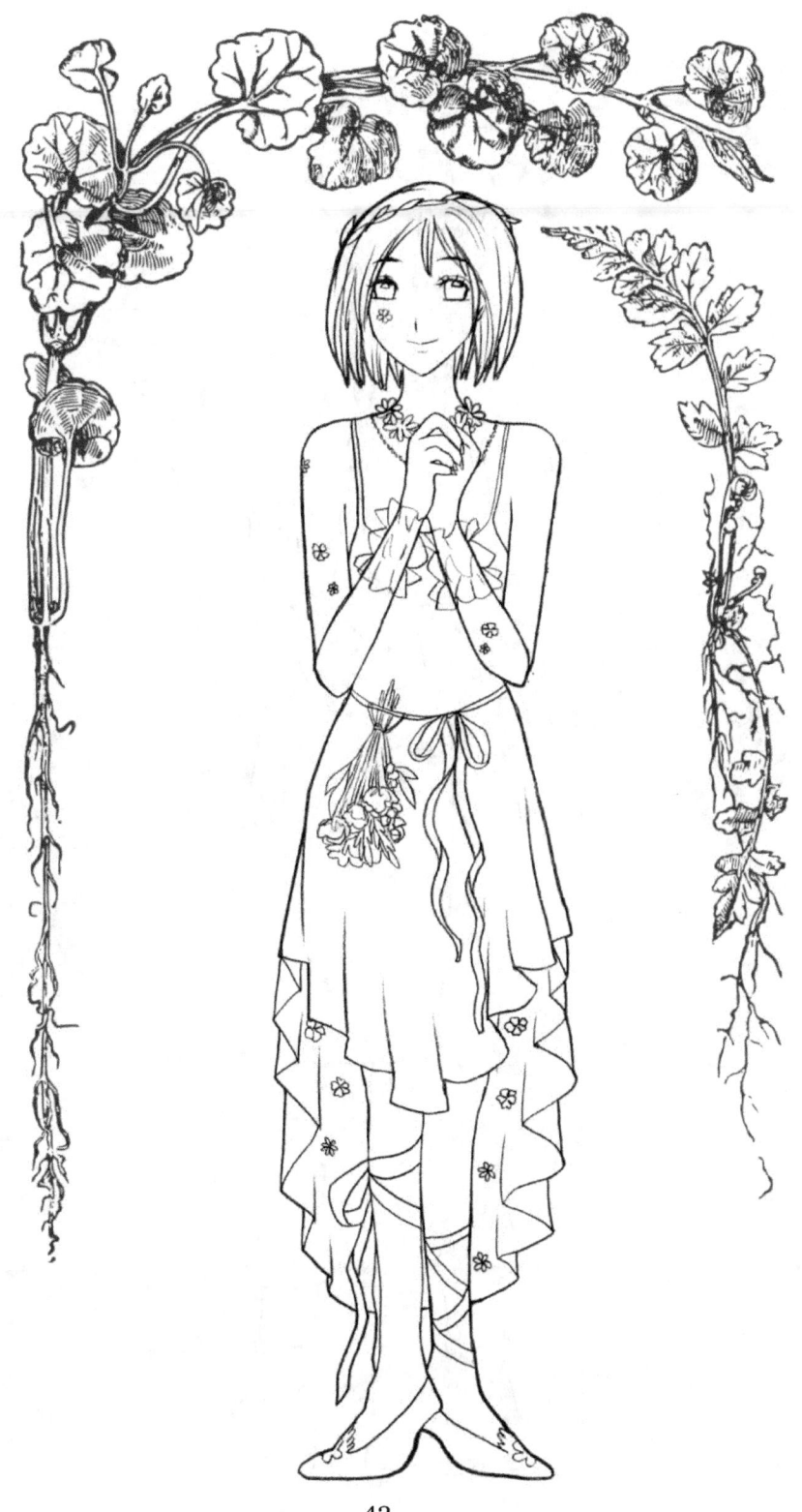

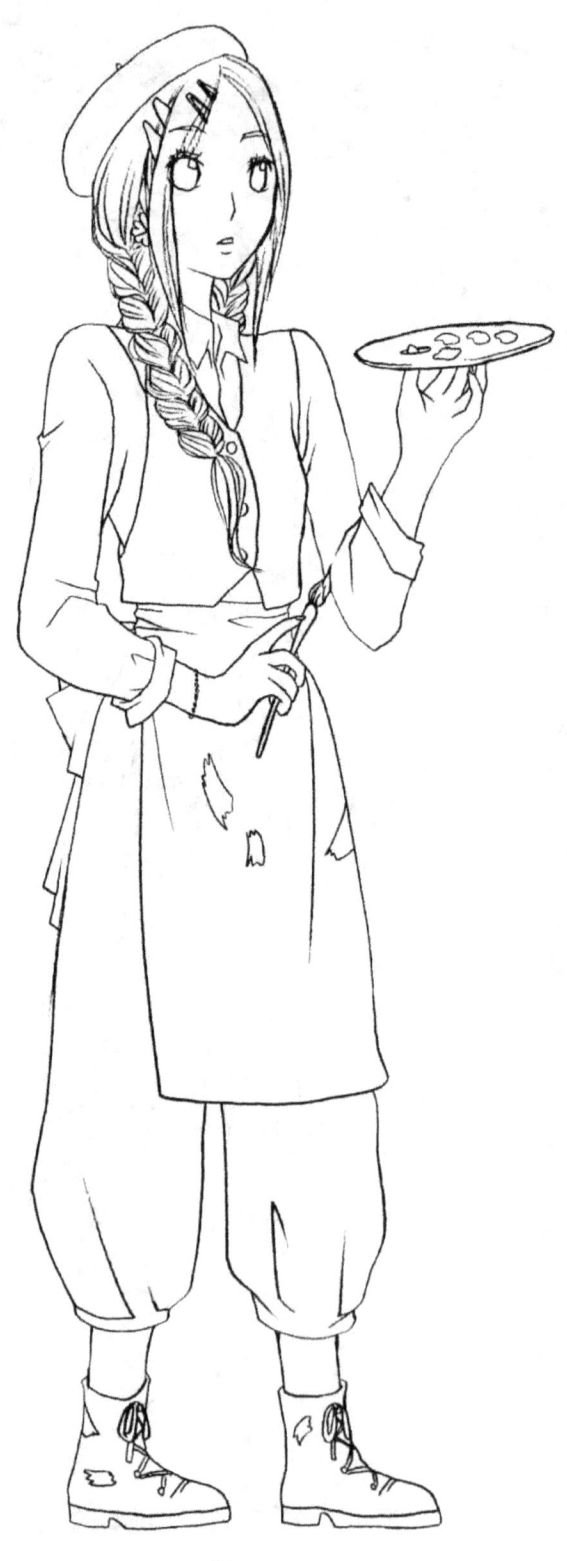

A picture of the future drawn in my dream
On the white canvas of my heart
Infused with lots of colors.
With my eyes open now,
I keep painting with those colors.

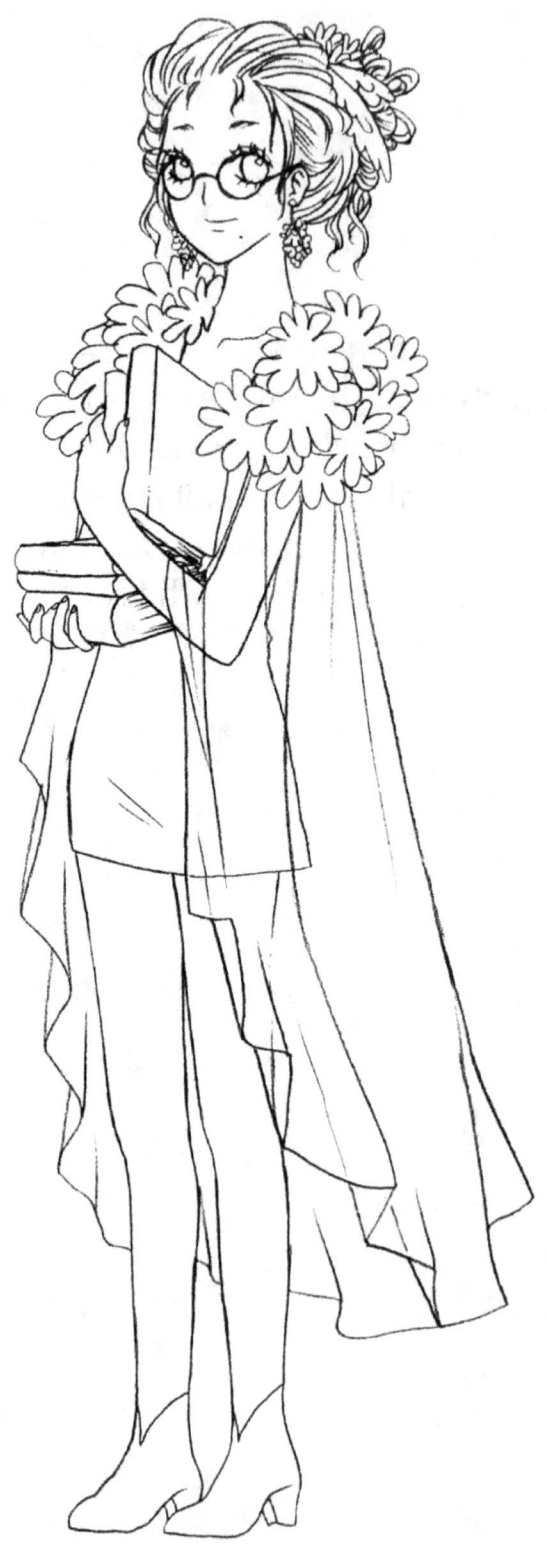

White birds fly in the sky
They bring love to someone
"Love and Growth"
Thanks to love,
That will help me grow
In the next season.

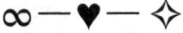

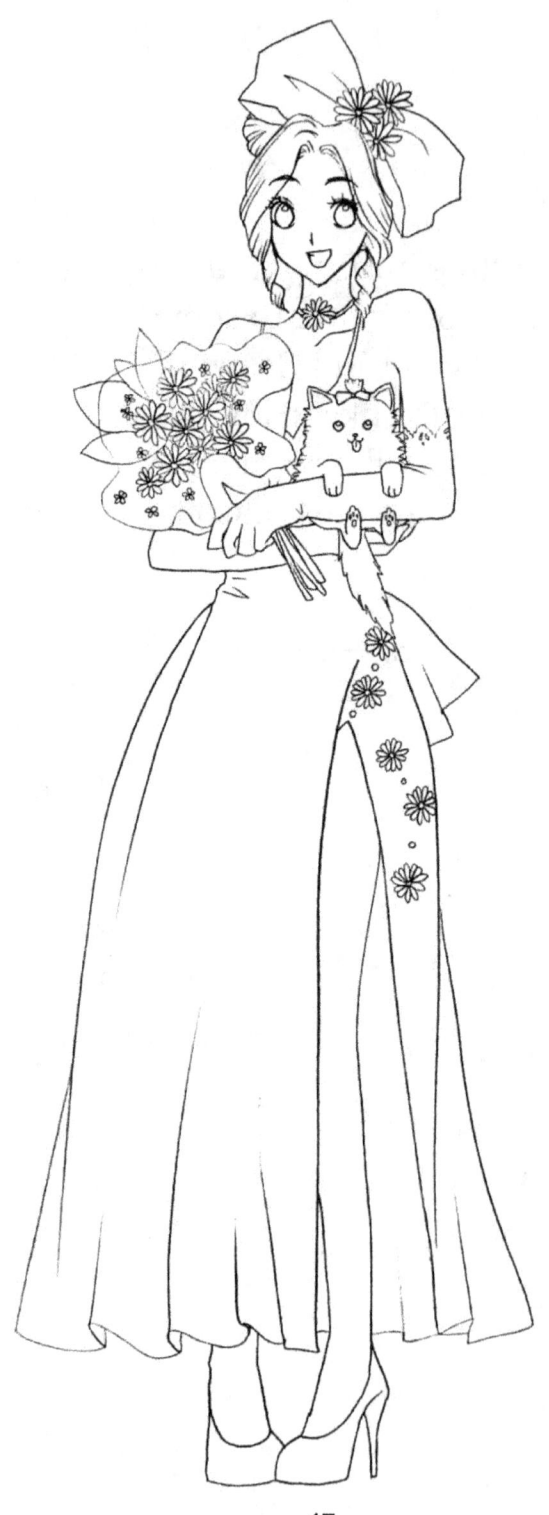

47

Things happen out of your mind.
Like fantasy becomes reality
Like a rainbow appearing in front of you
Happy thoughts and joy can create miracles.
So let's be happy!

Forget this and that
Forget who you are
And let's become an endless blue sky
Let's become a river that flows forever
Let's become a deep and vast sea
Because we're tiny things on earth,
Let's be what we love.

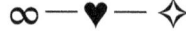

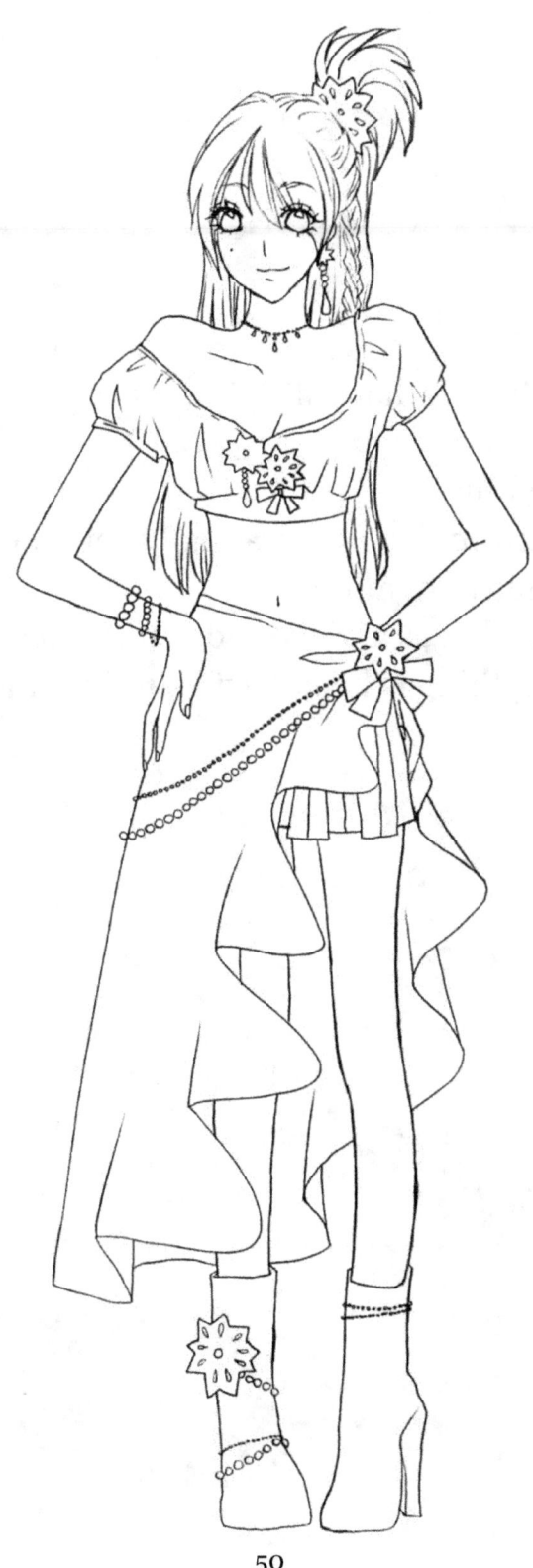

Someday, if I fall down, what will I do?
It might hurt.
I'm afraid of being hurt.
But after that, the wound would gradually get better.
Someday it won't hurt anymore.
Both wounds on my knees and wounds on my heart.
The day when everything is healed will surely come.

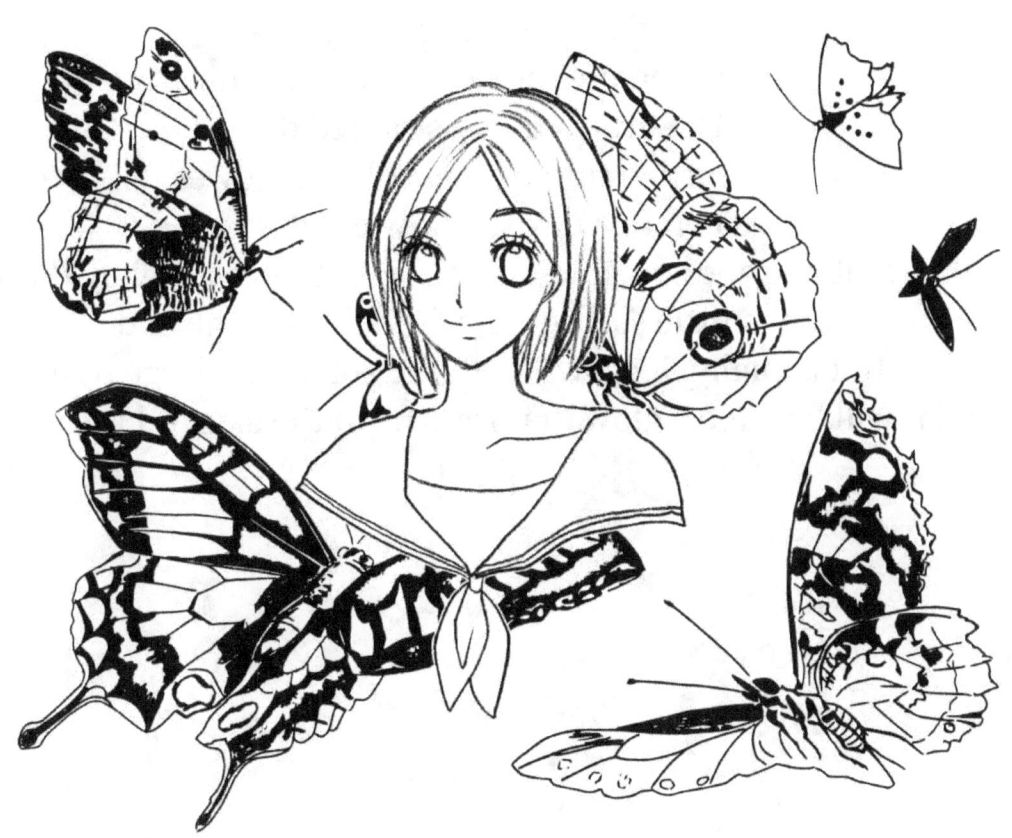

A star fell from the night sky
And became a seed that no one knows.
The little seed was rained down,
It turned into a cute, colorful flower.
Then one day the flower withered.
A part of it became soil, and another was blown away by the wind.
I'm a little sad because it looks like the end.
But actually, it grows from the soil into a large tree.
And it will become a glow that returns to the sky and the universe
again.

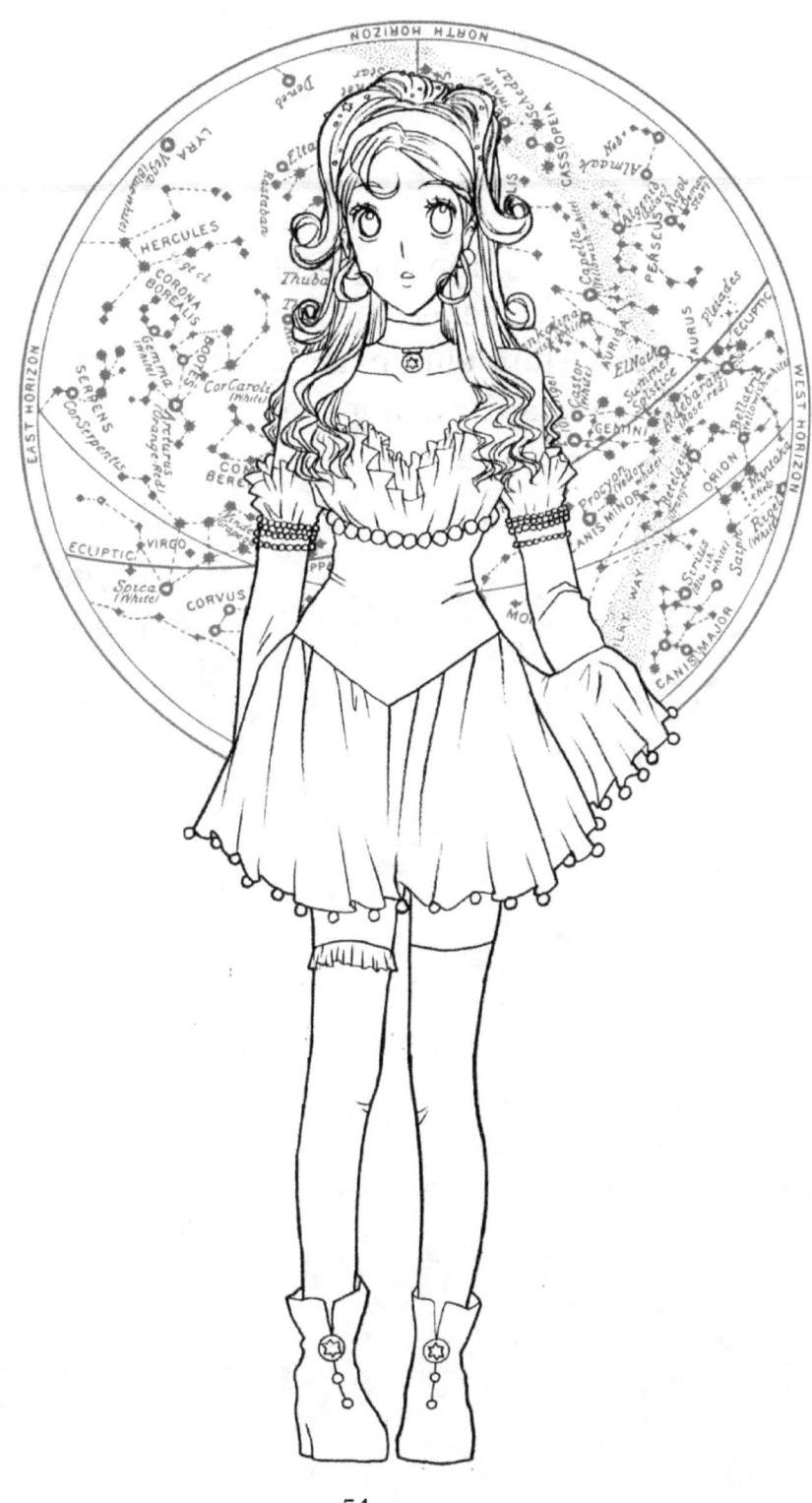

54

Hope is priceless.
It can be generated from our hearts.
Hope eliminates suffering.
We all have hope in ourselves.

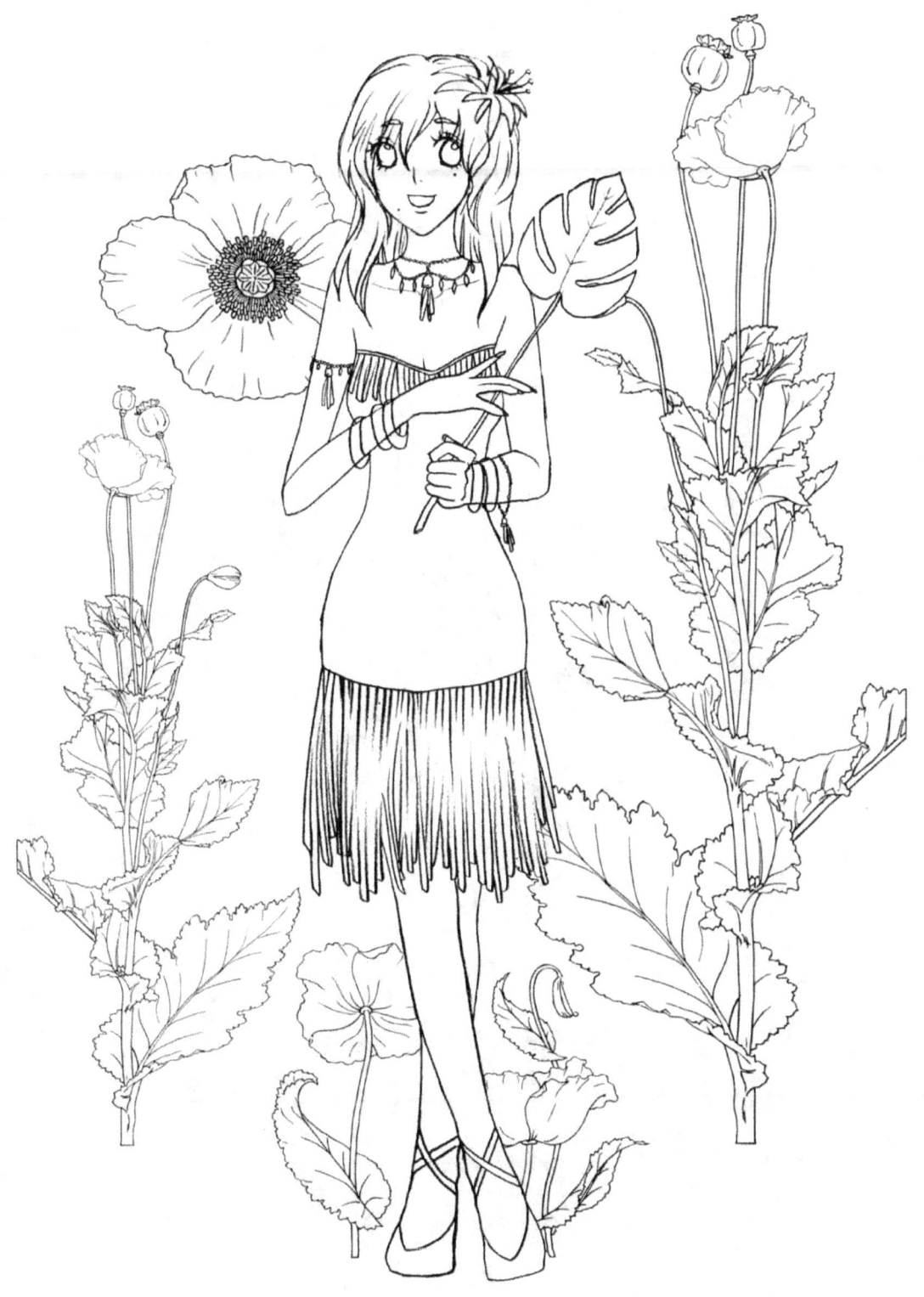

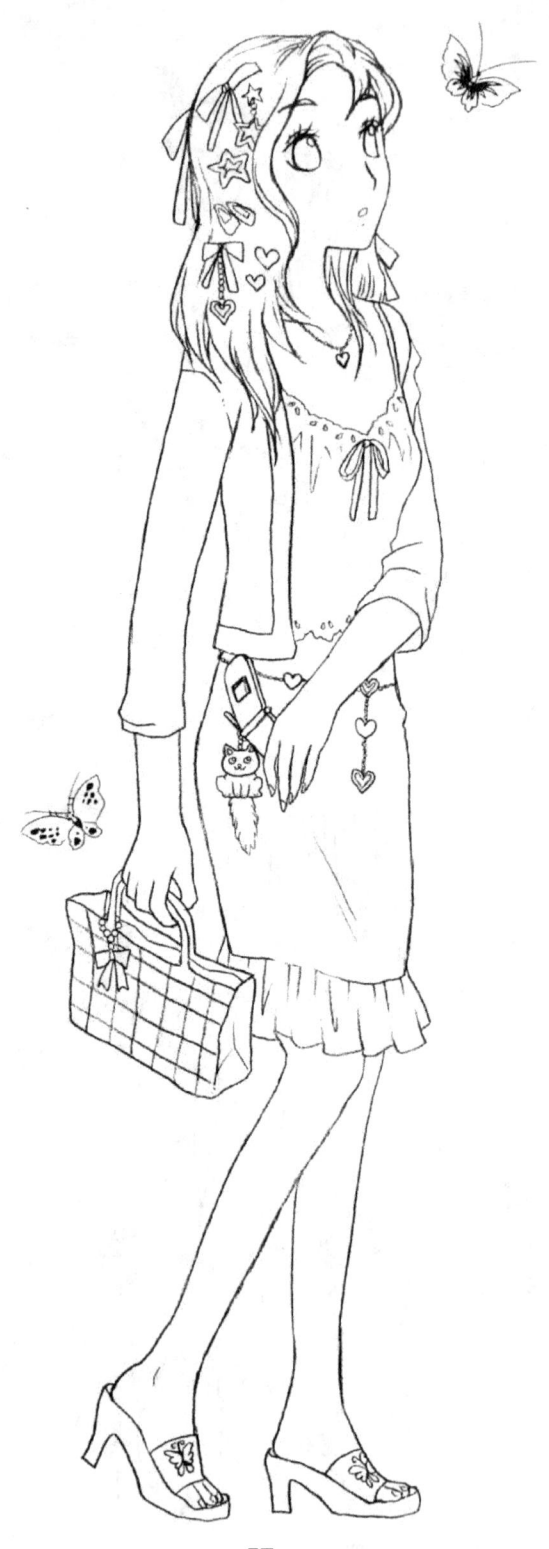

Spring butterflies are candy pink
The summer sea is baby blue
Autumn sweets are honey lemon
The winter scenery is daisy white

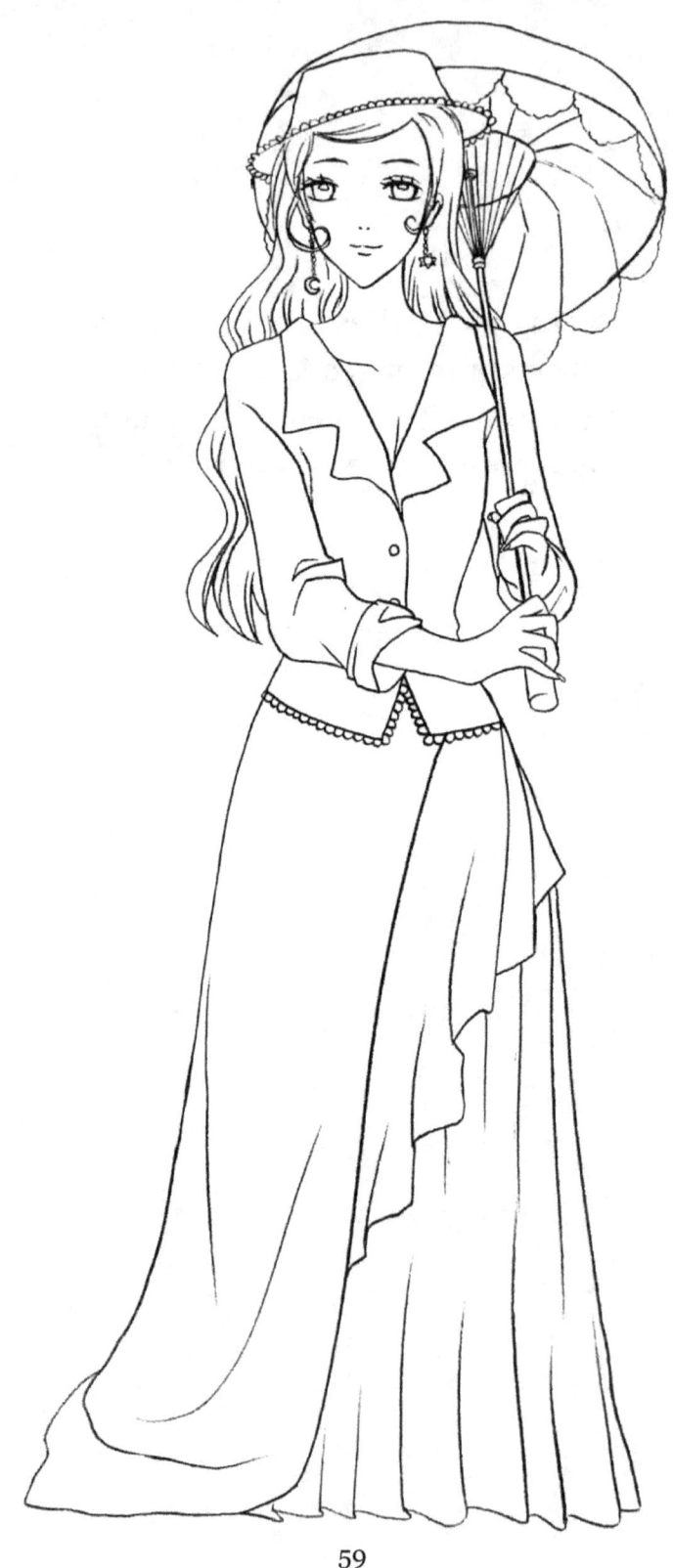

I write a love letter to you
I strew all tender words
About the fairy tale
That I saw in my dream.

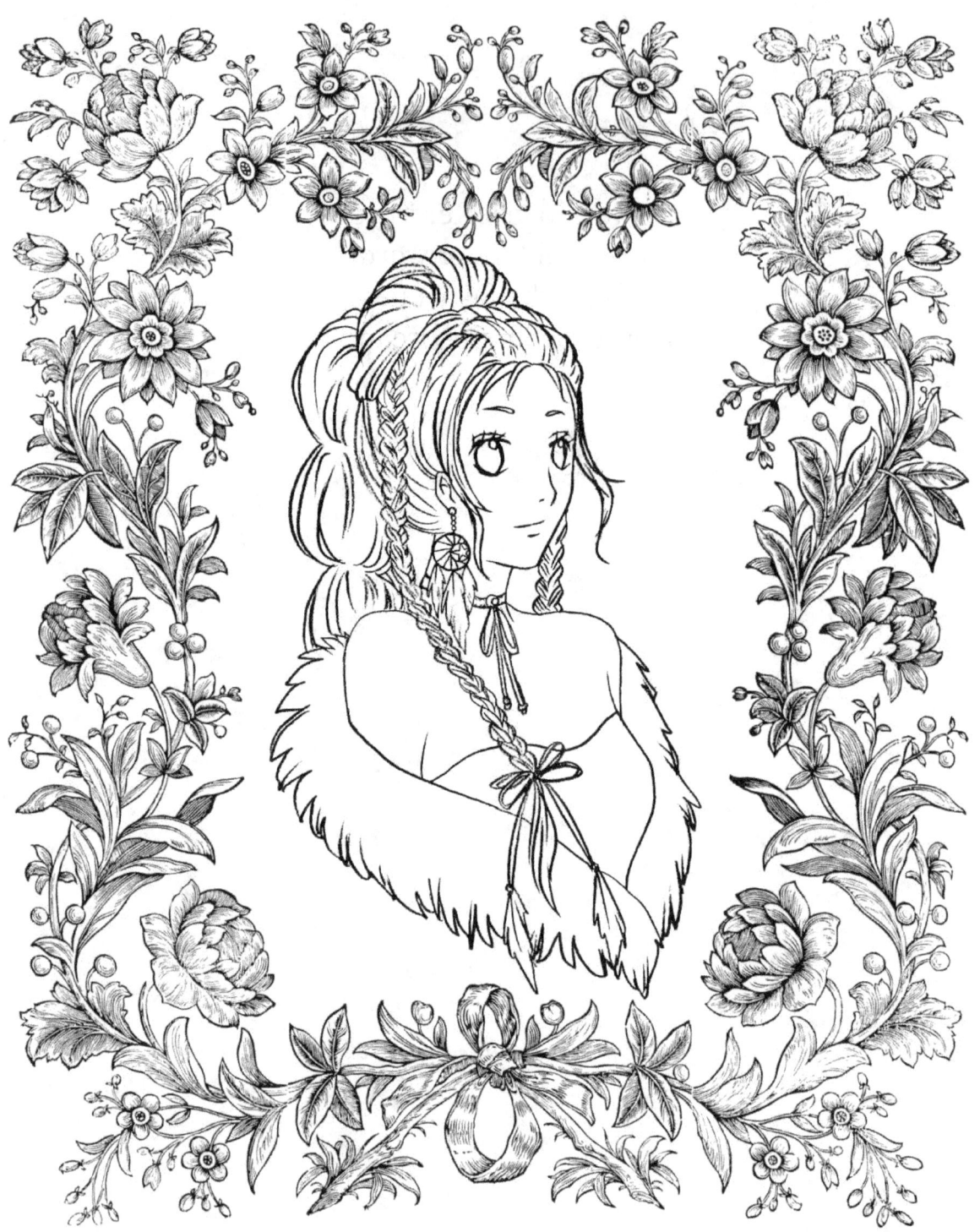

Mother Nature whispers to us
In our sleep,
"You're a good kid"
"Grow up happily"
"I will protect you."
She always gently embraces our spirits
With her large, transparent wings.

Tonight is the end of winter.
Everyone says goodbye.
Gray buildings were hidden
In the shadow of the moon
Like an illusion.
A century that hopes for the future
Is also waiting for the sun to rise again.

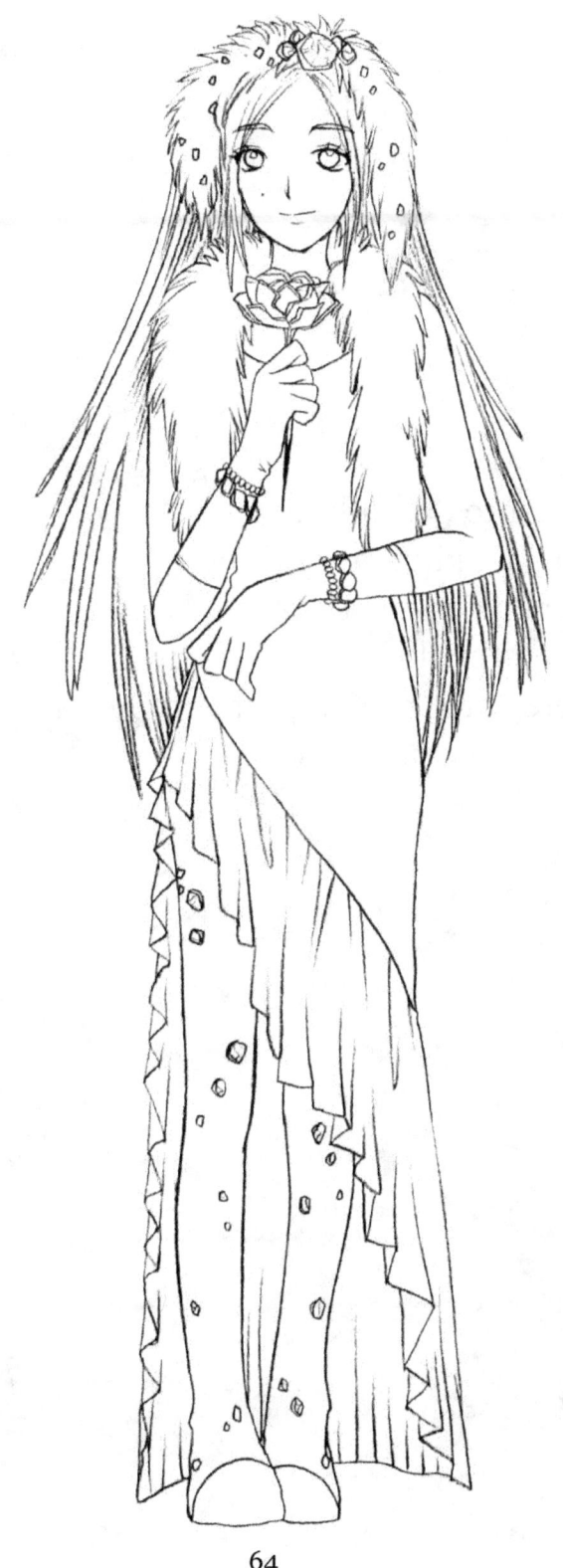

Sometimes it's best to do nothing.
Thinking nothing, looking for nothing
Like a half-read book on the table
Like clothes left on the floor
Escape from there with the wings of your heart
Let's fly off into the vast universe.

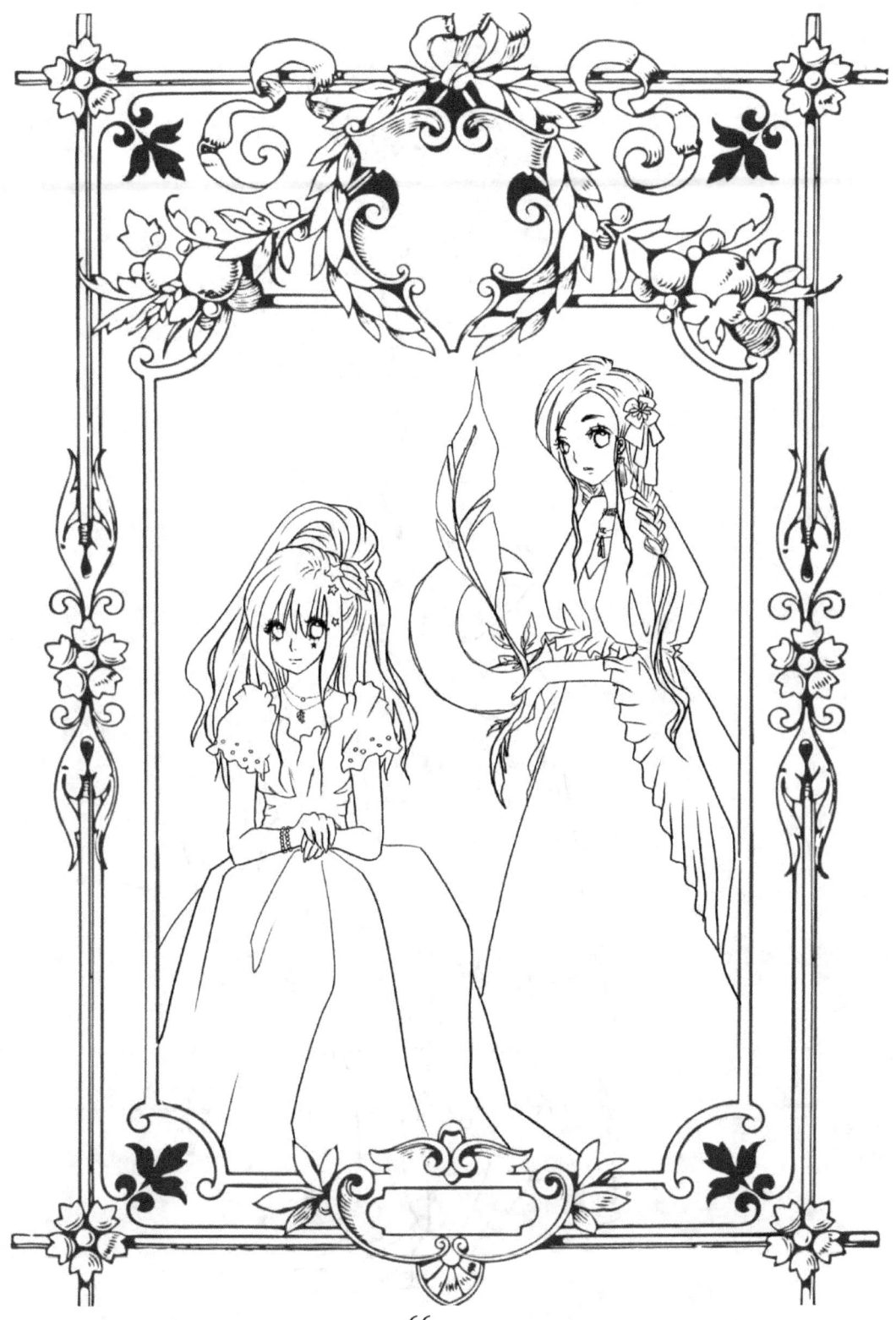

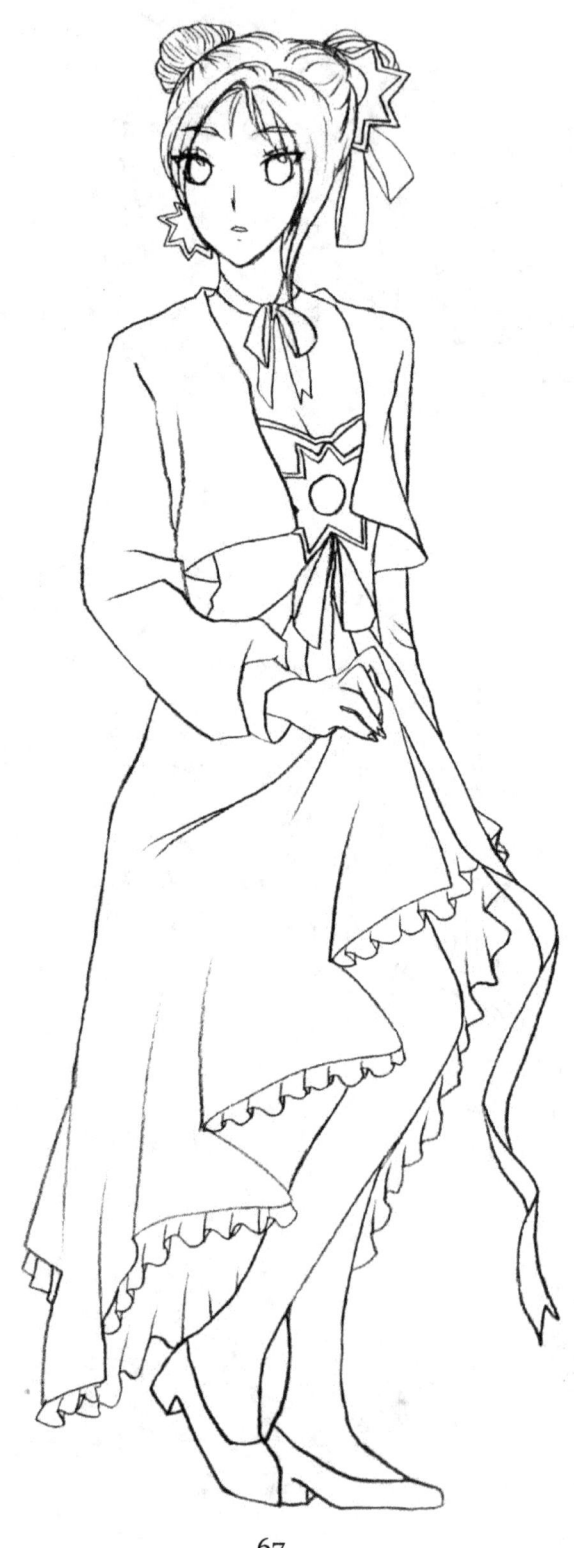

Let's travel to the moon
to find my future lover.
Even if it takes a long time,
I'll keep looking for that person.
But you know,
"Don't forget to love yourself even if you love someone else!"
"Never follow someone who doesn't love you as much as you do!"
That's what my mother told me.
Like she said, good things are worth waiting for.

Some words do not reach people even if they are translated.
Sometimes you can feel it without saying anything.
People are usually deeply and complexly connected with emotions.
The heart has no mouth, but it can communicate.

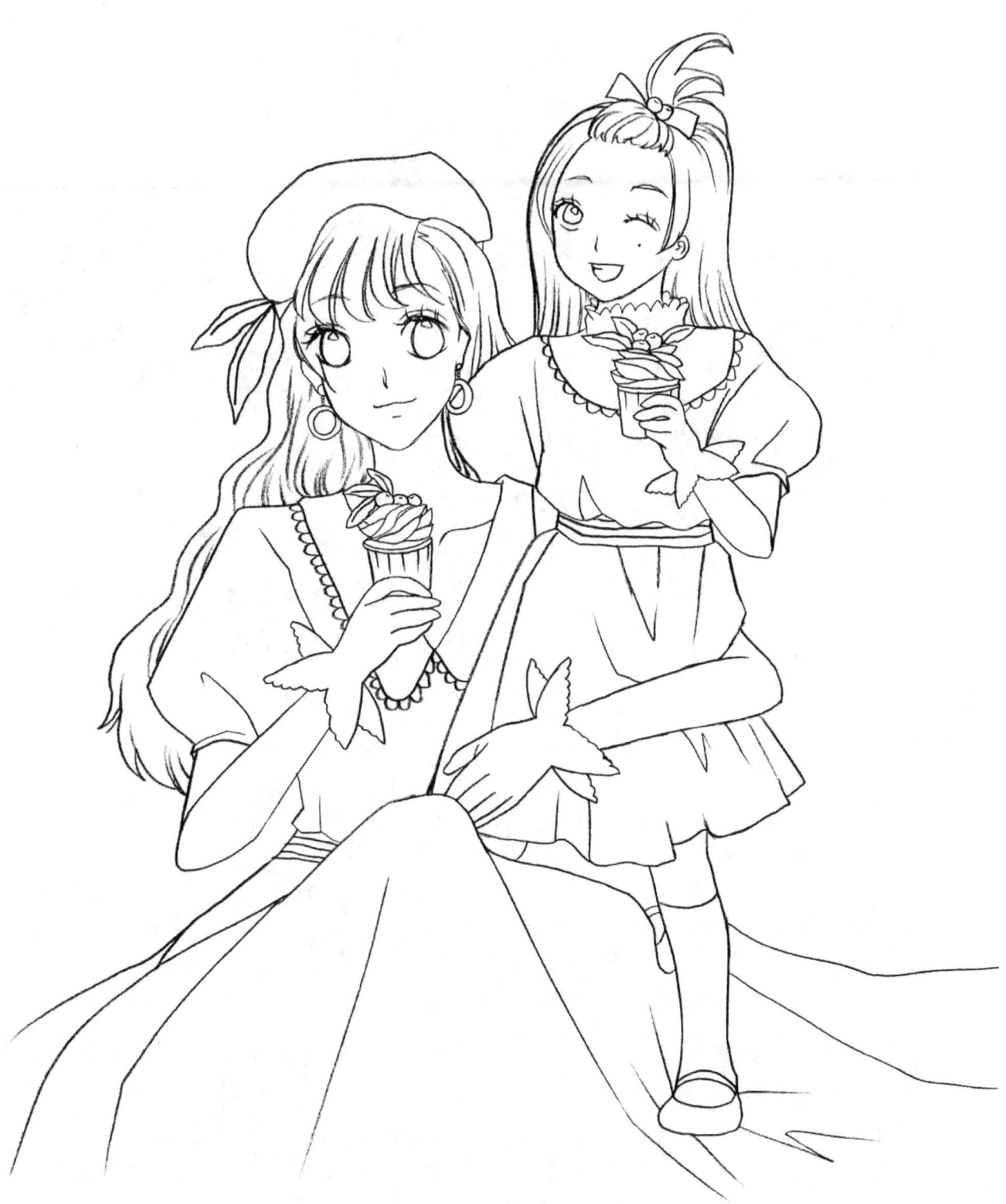

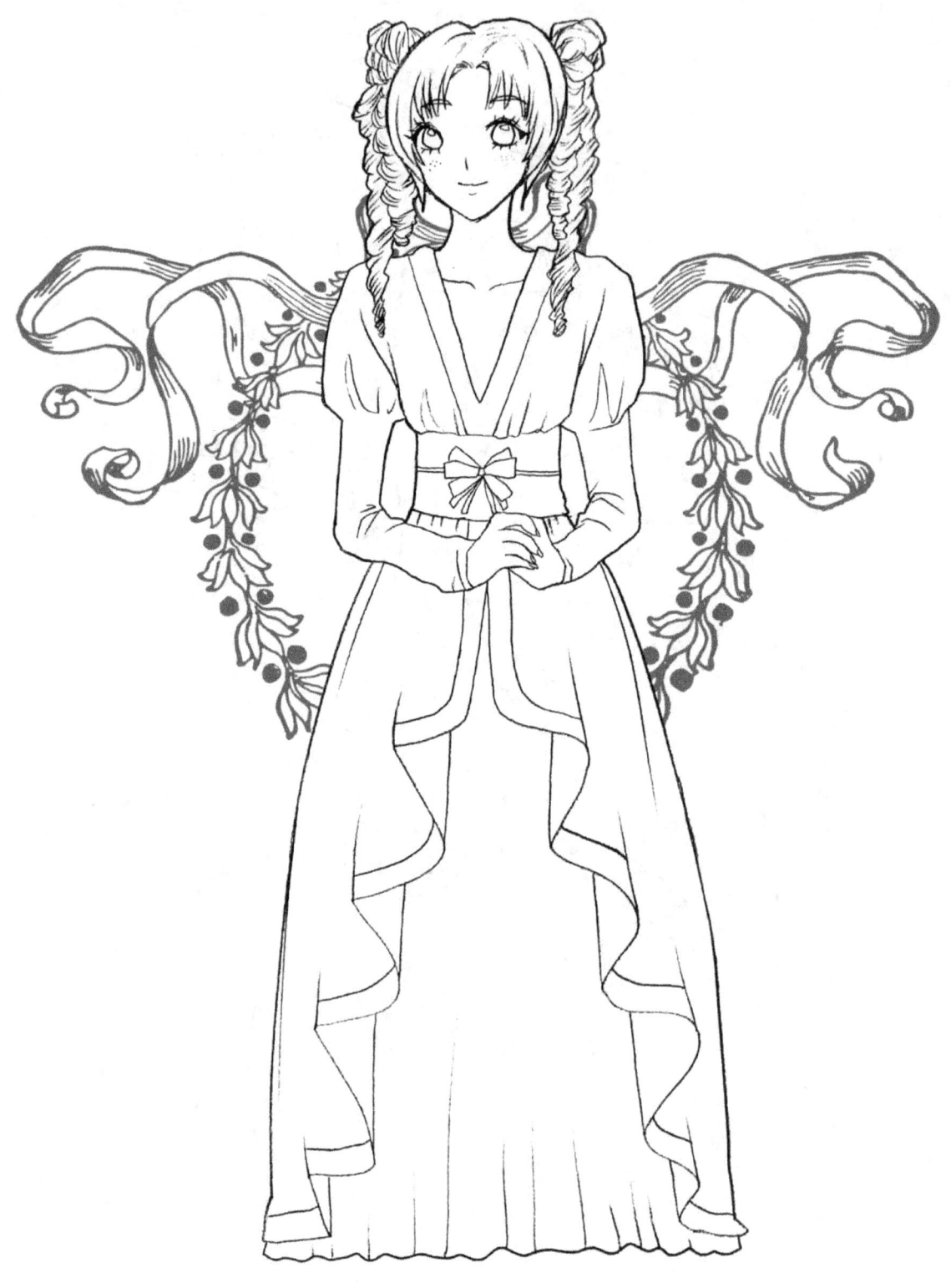

I gather the tears of my childhood,
And want to say to myself that
"It's fine"
"It's over."
As an adult, there were so many things came into my life,
But I'm glad I got over them.
So, I want to say
"All the struggles are gone"
"You don't have to cry anymore"
"Let's play"
"Let's be happy"
"You can do it now"
To me at that time.
The future I imagined at that time
Now it's shining right in front of me.

When I'm depressed, the question "Who am I really?" comes to mind.

To keep myself from getting lost any longer, I keep telling myself that "I used to be a magical girl before I became a working adult!" "I may look ordinary, but actually I'm a heroine!"

It might sound weird, but it literally gives my mind power back.

Whether you're a man or a woman, if you remember your hidden talents or childhood dreams, you'll find your self-esteem.

No matter how ridiculous the words are, if they give you courage, I think anything will do.

They are the magical words.

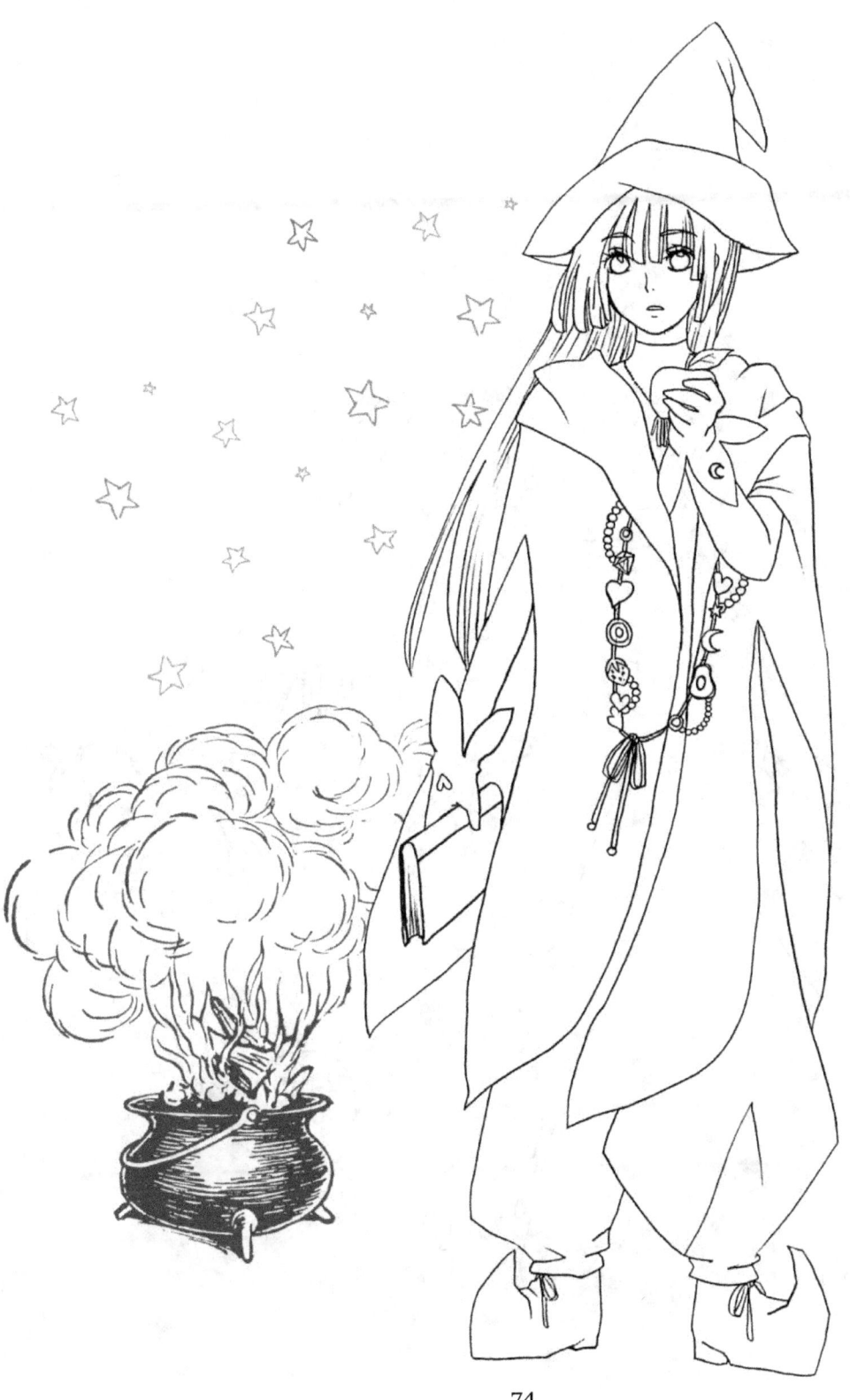

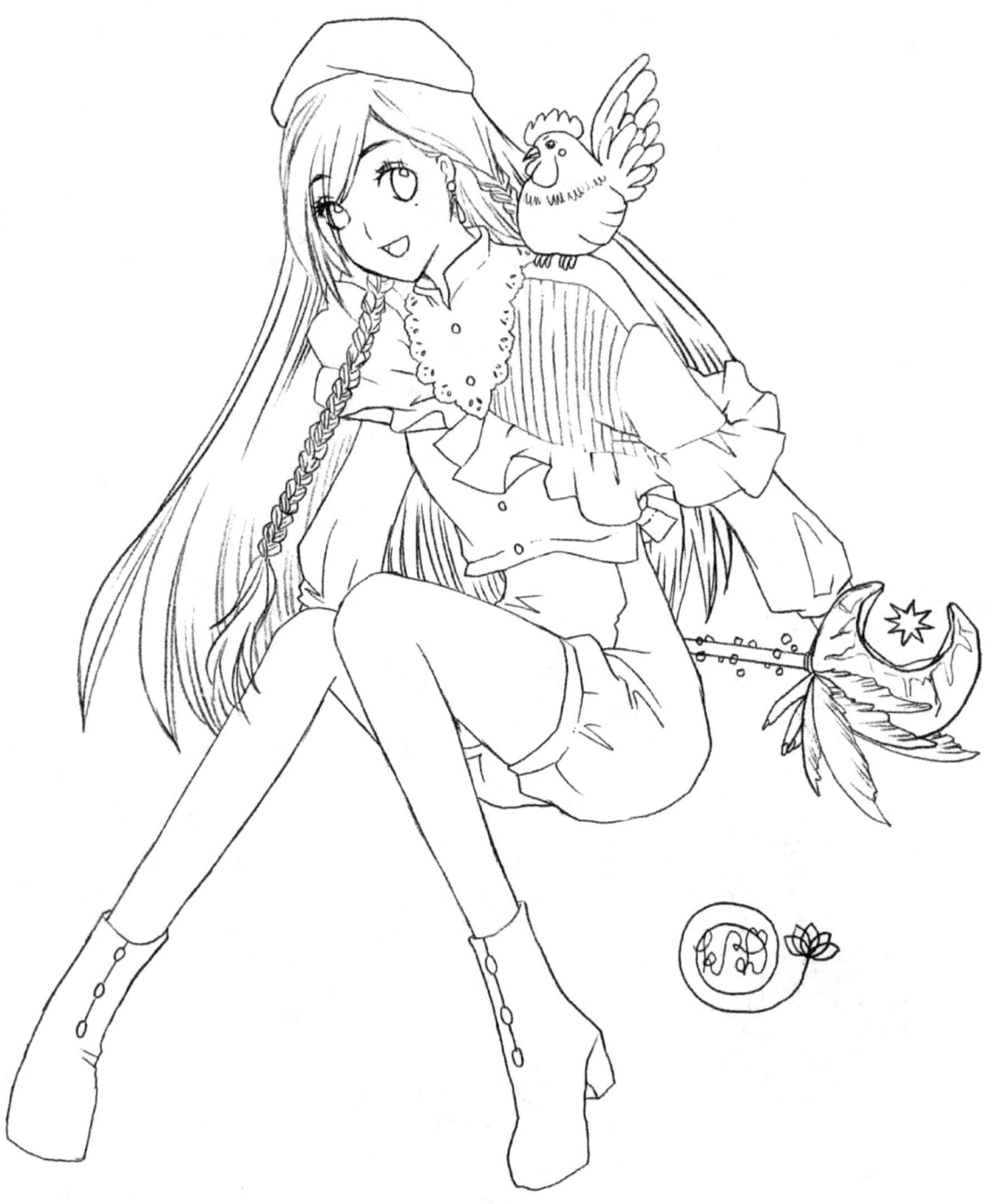

Let's get back to square one.
Let the rain wash everything away
and take a step towards a new, wonderful day.
The light in your heart always triumphs over the darkness.
No matter how old you are, don't forget your cheerful smile.
Let's make the world colorful again
with the colors that were sleeping in our dreams.
Believe in yourself and paint with your own happy color.

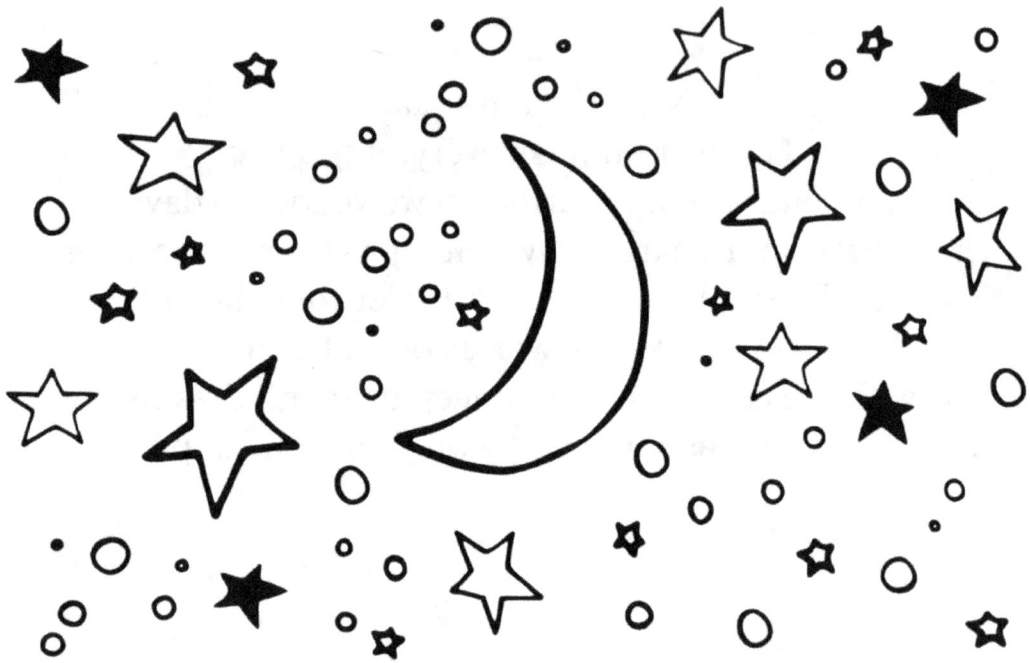

Let's send yourself a gift.
A pine tree decorated with glitter of the stars
A necklace encrusted with rainbow-colored gems
Colorful hydrangeas in full bloom during rainy season
A ticket to a dream paradise that only God knows

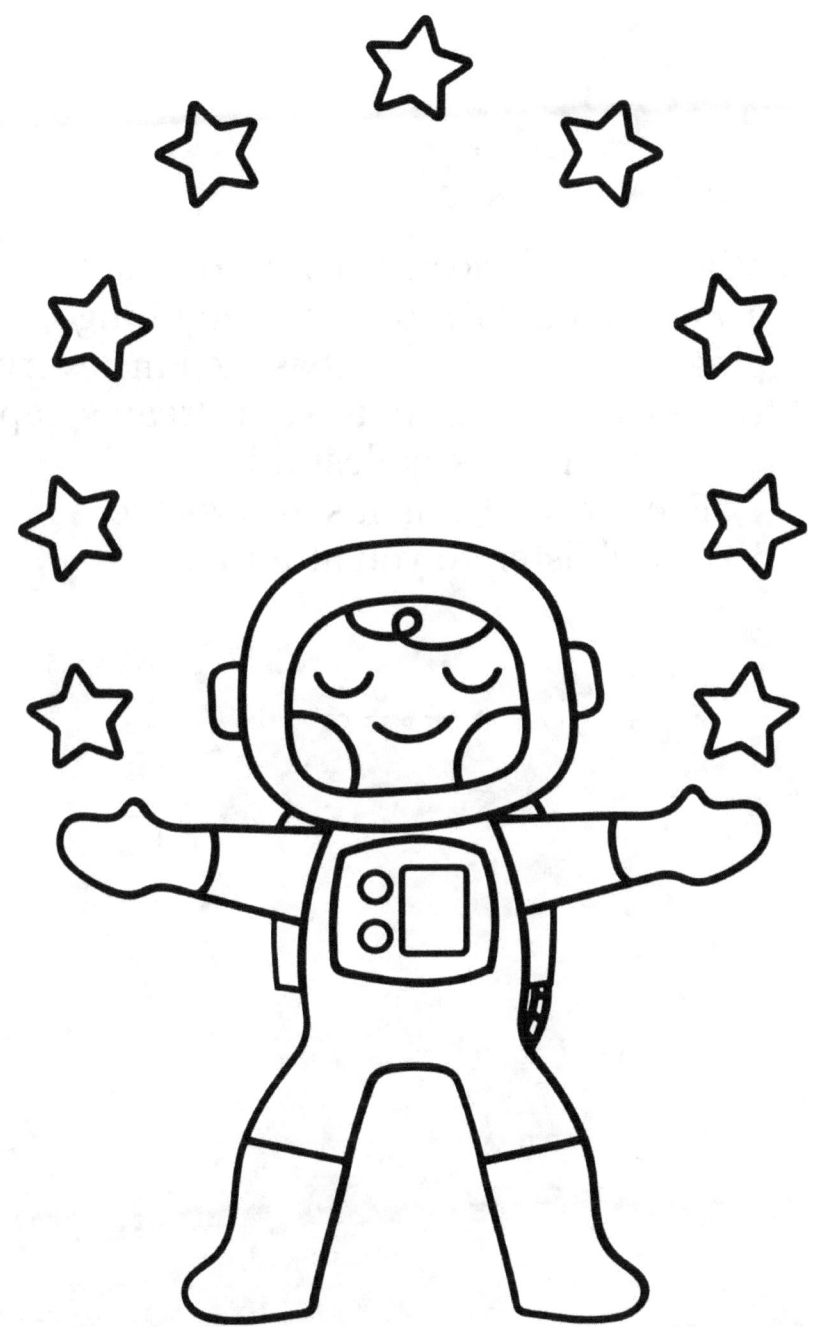

Can you tell me about your dream?
I want to hear it, so tell me anything.
I'm not going to judge you, so please tell me everything.
I want to see you talking about your dreams happily,
Even the smallest things
Even if you think it's impossible
I will listen to you attentively.

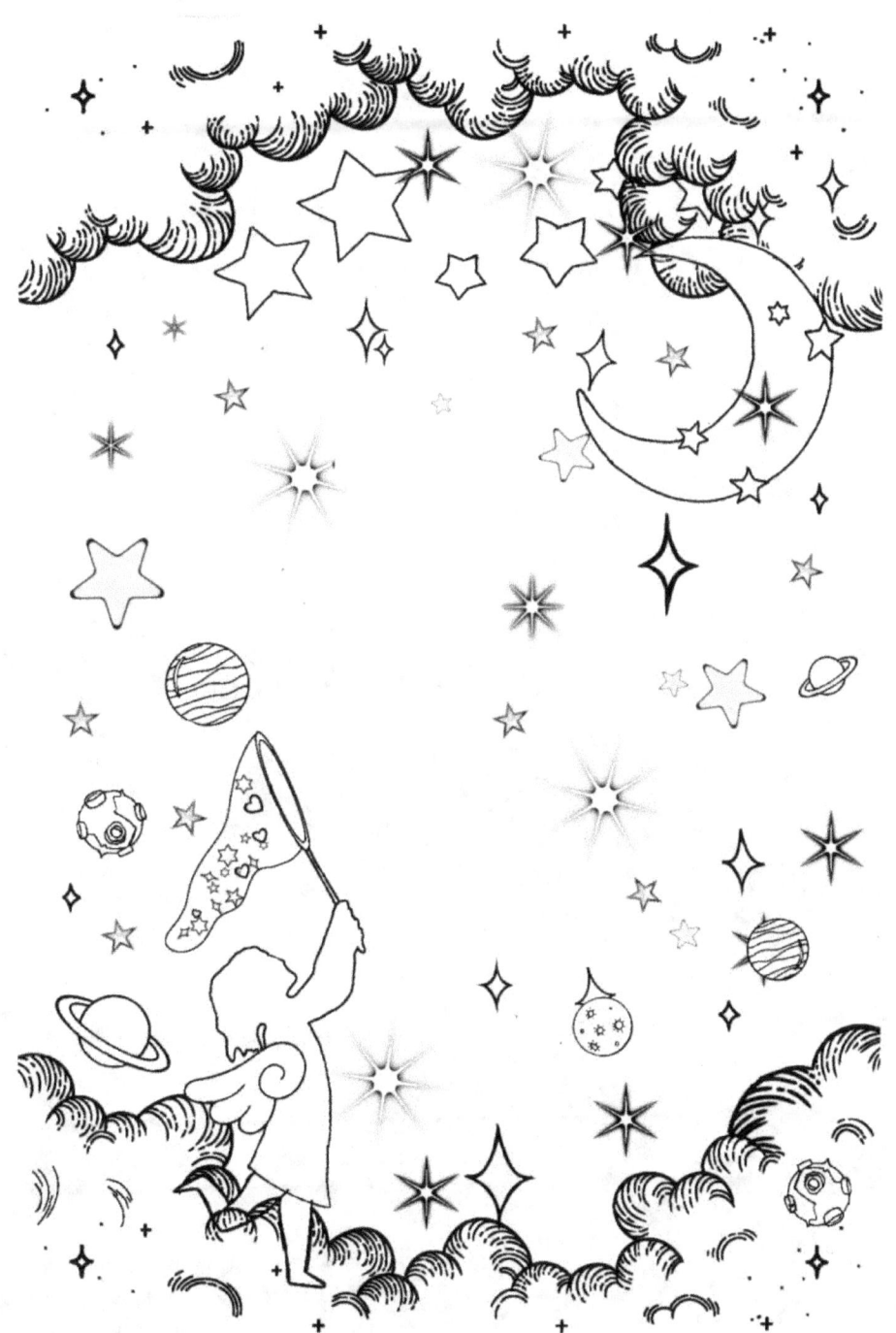

Epilogue

When I was a child, I was asked, "What do you want to be when you grow up?" I answered a nurse or an announcer randomly, but what I really want to be is "a magical girl".

At first, I thought that the definition of an "adult" was to abandon my childhood dreams. But now that I'm actually growing up, I've found that contributing to people with social responsibility and living happily without forgetting my favorite things and dreams like a child is my "definition of being an adult."

So, if you listen to your childhood voice and decide to plant a seed of happiness, you can be a magical girl at any age. I believe that "I can do everything" and "I can be everything" no matter how old I am, as long as my youthful heart is protected.

Karen Pink

Color your life
with the color of your childhood dreams
Coloring & Poetry book

Vol.1

By Karen Pink

About Author

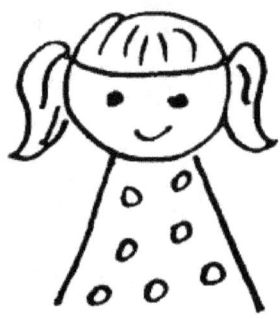

Karen Pink

Born in Bangkok on April 26th. After graduating from Chulalongkorn University's Department of Literature, she tried a variety of jobs, and she realized that the one that suited her best was the one that gave her freedom. She is currently working as a freelance translator, mainly at 'Amarin Printing and Publishing PLC.'

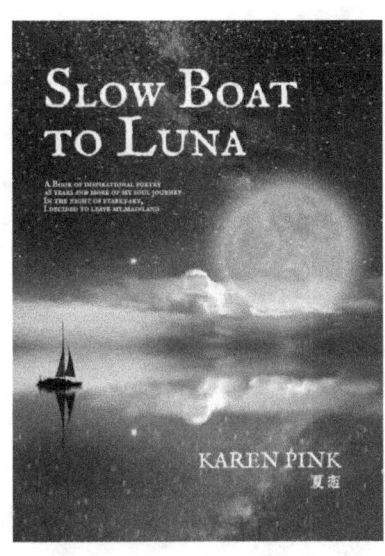

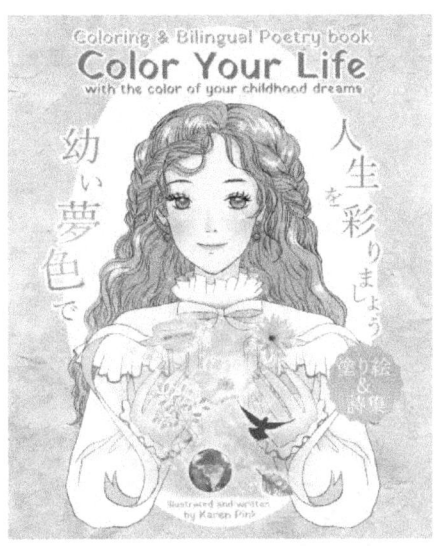

Slow Boat to Luna

Poetry & Illustration book
Published in 2022

Color Your Life Vol.2

Coloring & Poetry book
Published in 2023

www.ingramcontent.com/pod-product-compliance
Lightning Source LLC
Chambersburg PA
CBHW081626220526
45467CB00029B/3119